PELICAN BOOKS

Concepts of the Man-Made Environment
General Editor: Alexander Tzonis

Critical multi-disciplinary investigations
of fundamental problems in our environment.

THE MAN IN THE STREET

Shadrach Woods was born in New York in 1923. He was
educated at New York University College of Engineering and
Trinity College, Dublin. He began his architectural career in
Paris in 1948 where he worked at Le Corbusier. From Paris he
went to Algeria and Morocco and then in 1955 he became
principal of his own firm of architects based in Paris and
began to work throughout Europe. From 1962 onwards,
despite continuing with his design activities, he was Visiting
Critic in Architecture and Urban Design at a number of
universities in America and Europe. He lectured at a number of
architectural institutes throughout the world and also exhibited
his work at various universities in the United States and
Europe. His books include *Building for People* (1968),
Urbanism is Everybody's Business (1968) and *What U Can Do*
(1970).

From 1969 to 1973 Shadrach Woods was Professor of
Architecture at Harvard Graduate School of Design, and in
1973 he was appointed William Henry Bishop Visiting
Professor of Architecture, Yale University, but he declined this
post because of ill health. He died in the autumn of 1973.

9-4-76

SHADRACH WOODS

The Man in
the Street

A Polemic on Urbanism

PENGUIN BOOKS

ISBN

Penguin Books Ltd, Harmondsworth,
Middlesex, England
Penguin Books Inc., 7110 Ambassador Road,
Baltimore, Maryland 21207, U.S.A.
Penguin Books Australia Ltd, Ringwood,
Victoria, Australia

First published 1975

Printed in United States of America

Designed by Brian Folkard

Contents

Acknowledgements

For permission to use the illustrations in this volume acknowledgement is made to the following: Aerial Photos of New England, 10, 49; American Telephone & Telegraph Company, 32; Associated Press, Inc., 41; John Benson, 52; British Travel Association, 107; Henri Cartier-Bresson – Magnum, 106; Eugene Cook, 42; Leonard Freed – Magnum, 47; French Embassy Press and Information Division, 30; French Government Tourist Office, New York, 2, 6, 13, 84; Marc Garanger, 4, 5, 7, 9, 14, 15, 22, 24, 27, 31, 33, 34, 36, 86, 88, 89, 90, 102; Charles Harbutt – Magnum, 85; Harvard College Observatory, 1; Giraudon, 3; Jeff Gould – Gulf & Western Industries, 50; Italian Government Travel Office, New York, 29; Charles Jacob, 48; Karquel, 61; Litton Industries – Aero Service Division, 17; Sandra Lousada, 26, 28; Danny Lyon – Magnum, 104; National Council of Churches, 19; Netherlands Information Office, 51; Planned Parenthood – World Population Federation of America, Inc., 54; Prensa Latina – Photo Pascual, 56; Rijksmuseum, 53; Skyviews, New York, 87; David Kenneth Spector, 23; Vera Spoerri, 12; United Nations, 20, 39, 101, 115; US Department of Agriculture, 103; US Department of Transport, 25; H. Roger Viollet – Photo Albin Guillot, 40, 70; Windenberger, 37; Winkler, 55; Yan, 91; Raimond dit Yvon, 35; Yugoslav Information Center – Photo Vilko Zuber, 46.

The following plans and diagrams are reproduced with permission of Shadrach Woods; 11, 38, 57, 58, 59, 60, 61, 62, 63, 64, 65, 66, 69, 70, 71, 72, 73, 74, 75, 76, 77, 78, 79, 80, 81, 82, 83, 92, 93, 94, 95, 96, 97, 98, 99, 100, 108, 109, 110, 111, 112, 113.

Drawings 67 and 68 are by Joachim Pfeufer; montage 93 is by Waltraude Schleicher. Population distribution in the Paris area, diagram 16, appeared in *L'Usine nouvelle*, February 1968, p. 107. The cartoon reproduced as illustration 8 is by Bill Maudlin and it appeared in the *Chicago Sunday Times*, 1966.

Introduction:
What is the Problem?

Decline in the west has long been a subject of fascination as well as an established phenomenon. Among its many expressions, the deterioration of cities seems to me to carry the most significance. The city of man ('Oh, what a beautiful city!' as the gospel song has it) has surely been one of civilization's finest accomplishments; it has often, and usually, appeared as an ideal for 'civilized' man, and has been, in fact, the only seat of civilization and the base of its power. In the past, most often, 'great' or 'mighty' were the adjectives to qualify cities.

In the past two centuries ideal cities have been a source of inspired speculation, imagined as the perfect containers for ideal societies. A direct connection could readily be assumed between urban form and political system, indeed such a connection was evident in history. Now, when we continue to speculate today about urbanism and its predictable effects, we are continuing in a certain tradition. That tradition comes to us from many sources (for example, the Fourierists) who projected urbanistic correspondencies for reformed societies. We might choose another example; there were many in that 'enlightened' time. If we choose Charles Fourier and his disciples to illuminate this point, it is because Fourier seems to us to be closer to the socialism which eventually dominated the early twentieth-century urbanism than many of the others,* who perhaps were more ideological and less socialistic.

In nineteenth-century urban planning the goals of social and political organization were seen to correspond closely to the forms and the functions of the city, as indeed, had been the case in preceding societies, however less ideal. The city, functioning sweetly, was,

* We are thinking, for instance, of Robert Owen.

1. *We may look, for instance, to the Fourierists who projected urban-istic correspondences for reformed societies.* General view of a Phalanstery, or corporate village, organized on the theory of Fourier. Drawn by Jules Arnot, after the plans of Morize.

and was to be, the demonstration as well as the support of our collective will to live together in harmony. Thus, social and economic parity could be both exemplified by, and lodged in, perfectly designed buildings within limpid urban organizations, all postulated and programmed through a total reorganization of society. None of this actually happened, and that is disappointing to us, the north European descendants of the genitors of those marvelous humanist schemes.

In the time of that vast and far-reaching social revolution, which began with Voltaire and ended with Napoleon, many schemes were produced to suit ideal societies. Social (or societal, as we say today) reconsideration generated architectural and urbanistic speculation. Among other examples of architectural speculation, such as Claude Nicolas Ledoux and Boullée, the work of Charles Fourier appears to us as being the most interesting at that time. Fourier will serve as our illustration of how urbanism and architecture were incorporated into a social reformist movement. It should not be inferred that Fourierist theories are applicable to our time, nor that Fourier had any grasp of theories applicable beyond his own parish. He did however, promulgate a life style, complete with adequate architecture, for a new man in that time. It is always difficult for the persons in place to imagine how necessary changes might be made in order to change, gracefully, from one social order to the next. There is sometimes a continuum which we call culture, which will haltingly carry us over the difficult passages. The use of this device, the support of continuing culture (i.e. the past achievements of any race), was very much a part of Fourier's scheme for revitalizing social interaction in the brand new world. Like any reasonable planner he looked to the treasury of acquired social interaction, and built from that. He sought out the best of what existed in his revolutionary world and tried to mix the old wine and the new bottles. Thus, in addition to the physical planning of new communities, time slots were allocated for diverse, revitalizing activities for the members of the communities. It should be noted that the time spent, over all, added up to the time needed for the pursuit of each activity under the old system. Fourier was not yet threatening to 'turn it around' in terms of the society at large; he was only trying to sort out the individual's relationship to society. In a sense, he was saying that reform, at the individual level, might promise a considerable transformation of the entire society.

The very idea of using time in order to diversify the pursuits of the persons who make up a society, for instance, seems even today a revolutionary notion. The butcher, the baker, the candlestick maker, become interchangeable parts. No one is condemned to the life of a single occupation, unless he wishes to be. Normally this should be a liberating force. Since all of Fourier's ideas were normative, people would be liberated, like it or not, from their previous mono-occupational state. There was to be, in Fourier's intent, a complete and profound intellectual investigation of what people ought to be doing with their lives, and how architecture and planning could best be used to further that ideal concept. Thus, built environments, called Phalansteries, would be erected to accommodate the new man in his daily pursuits. This, we must admit, was a stupendous conceit, the product of an extraordinary intelligence. It contained a clear vision of the necessity as well as the possibilities of a total integration of the physical, social and temporal milieus into one habitat. It was overtaken and rendered obsolete (in the details but not necessarily in the concept) by the massive movements of population which came with the Industrial Revolution.

Fourier's ideas, which were not so much his alone as those of his epoch, were obscured in the dust raised during the conversion from a rural to an urban economy and from a parochial to national hierarchy in France, and only some timid examples of his phalansteries survive in the mid-eastern states of North America, along with other communes (inspired or demented) of the nineteenth century. None of these carry any significance for our society today, apart from their historical value or exemplary content for contemporary drop-outs. However one may greatly regret the occasion which was lost to us when Fourierism fell a victim to another kind of progress. The world (the western world, naturally) was not then ripe for such radical ideas of harmony and goodness; will it ever be? One may question whether men, at least within the western tradition, will ever be able to live with the idea that they are essentially good, or with the idea of living together, cohabiting in community. It is always much easier to destroy such ideas than to act them out. The essential instrument of destruction is the self-fulfilling prophecy, loaded with the dire warnings of man's essential badness. Then we reject the good, and live, so to speak, with the bad that we know is in us. And indeed, we have come to compete to prove how bad we can be. Fourier and his disciples envisioned a world in which we would not need to compete, since we would all be, basically, good. This may sound ludicrous, but perhaps only to our super-civilized tin ears. We should remember that much of Fourier's thought (along with the thought of Marx and Engels) has been resuscitated and rehabilitated as doctrine in the expanding socialist world. We may yet see the modern equivalents of Fourier's phalansteries in South America, Africa or Asia. We may still take hope, since nothing in the realm of ideas is ever lost.

In clearly structured, tyrannical societies preceding this time of

2. *In the clearly structured, tyrannical societies which preceded this time of enlightened speculation, it was normal and natural to express and to reinforce the hierarchy of authority through public buildings and the organization of the city.* View of the palace at Versailles.

enlightened speculation it was certainly normal to express and to reinforce the hierarchy of authority through urban design and the design of specific building (e.g. Peking, Versailles). Urban clarity reflected a rigid, well-organized, comprehensible and highly repressive political system, with power, at the expense of the individual, concentrated in a central authority. It is highly unlikely, moreover, that any question of individual social or psychological cost was ever raised. When the very concepts of social mobility and personal freedom of choice are virtually unknown, unthinkable for the society at large, it would be difficult to imagine that the embryo citizens (still subjects) could consider the urban environment as an instrument of repression. In fact, the king, the emperor, the pope or the prince was in his place (his palace) at the heart of the city, from which source all power flowed forth, and was channeled into a system – a network – hallowed by tradition and social structure, and firmly established to support a superstructure of vested interests. The plan of the city was centered, ideally, upon the facts and the symbols of authority; it was static by the nature of its representative intent. The plan had no potential for change and indeed, it was clear that it should never change. There was total interdependence among the economic, political, social and spatial organizations which structured the city and the state, and which contributed to its continuing functioning. Thus the monumental intent of urban design can be viewed as a kind of political functionalism. The scale of the city was such that its organization could be symbolic and immediately comprehensible. Even its embellishments were functional, intended to reinforce the ideal of central authority. The centralized and monumental nature of planning and urban design was not merely an intellectually satisfying and comprehensible aesthetic device; it was also a direct translation of political reality into the physical environment, art holding a mirror up to nature.

Political and social thinkers of the last two centuries quite naturally postulated the same interdependence of political, socio-economic and spatial organizations in their schemes for a new, less arbitrary, urban society. Clear urban networks, often surprisingly non-centric, were offered as the physical counterparts of their rational political and social systems. The heady new wine of social and political reform was not to be contained in the old, musty bottles. However, despite the tempting delights of rationalism, the massive commitment and investment which the existing cities represented, both in terms of culture and finance, proved even more powerful than

3. *However, despite the tempting delights of rationalism, the massive commitment and investment proved to be even more powerful than the force of those powerful dreams ... and the new, open political systems would have to be accommodated in the old, closed urban form.* Gustave Doré: Les Embarras de la circulation à Londres, or traffic problems in London about a hundred years ago.

the force of those powerful dreams. For reasons of expediency the new, open (or potentially open), political systems would have to be accommodated within the old, closed urban form. The new city, in Europe at least, was not to be, and from that time the need for the man in the street to be concerned about urbanism has existed. Every new idea was a flower on the dung-heap of repressive urban design.

In the newly colonized countries, notably the Americas, the opportunity to redesign urban structures abounded and was thoroughly exploited, especially by the colonial bureaucracies at home. City plans were conceived as matrices for the subdivision of land, and thus were generally open and non-centric, in their form, if not in their intent. Unfortunately these plans, the Quadras of Latin America and the grids of North America, accompanied outrageous instances of colonial exploitation and cultural annihilation. Those open plans were to accommodate a hermetically closed society. They seemed a transplantation, or a translation, into bureaucratic language of a reasonable and just social ideal. The European oligarchies of North and South America were not at home in them, although they have set a kind of style for urban design in the New World (as opposed to the new world) for which we may yet be grateful. Unwittingly perhaps the colonialists of America have given America a head start toward the realization of appropriate urban structures for an open society. There are few Versailles on the American continents and the culture shock produced on the colonists and aborigines alike, by these rationalist grid-iron plans may yet prove to be more of an asset than a liability in urban development in these countries where the concept of monumental, representative, oppressive urban design is practically unknown. That is to say, that within the grid plan common to most cities of America, no one really knows how to reproduce the awe and stately grandeur of Versailles, or Peking, or Moscow, or even Paris. The United States has wrestled, unavailingly, with this problem for many years, always without admitting what the problem was. All efforts to turn the grid into a princely city fall short, since none but the private developers can ever reassemble large tracts of land on which to carry out an urbanistic exercise of this nature. And private developers are not much interested in urban symbolism.

Meanwhile, in northern Europe, where the political correspondences for these open, non-centric plans were coming into being, cities were losing their symbolic functions as their hierarchical structures dissolved, under the impact of an influx of population from rural areas. There was a loosening of the old political and economic structures, a new organization of activities and a shift of population from rural to urban centers. The cities grew in population at a fantastic rate and, at a time when they most needed an organizing authority, authority was being dissipated as the existing political hierarchies were being overthrown.

As the cities were being overwhelmed and overcrowded, their power to rule themselves was being dissipated. As the obvious connections between the city and its environs became more evident, the concentration of power within the hands of a limited ruling circle, within the city, was disputed more and more successfully. Thus Paris became the capital of France, but it also became the largest Savoyarde or Auvergnate city. The Savoyards and the Auvergnats quickly organized themselves (these examples are valid for all western capitals) and became a divisive force to be reckoned with. They became important as political entities within the system of the city. They were not of the city, although they were in the city. The rules of the game had to change since, although not much could be done with them, nothing could be done without them. They appropriated the city and tried to remake it to correspond more closely to their ideal. Since their ideal, at first, was still rooted in Savoie, or Auvergne (Rastignac was an exception), the result was a chaos of petty politics and influence peddling which haunts us even today. In North America where cities are new, we can still practice ethnic politics at the city scale. Nothing melts in the melting pot: ethnic background still determines entry into many activities, not by law but by tradition, and politicians are required to make obeisance to the curious notion of national or racial origin, almost before any position on issues can be taken.

Cities, old and new, have had to englobe, but have rarely assimilated, succeeding waves of immigration. People uprooted, for reasons beyond comprehension, cannot be expected to reroot in a totally foreign jungle. They seek, as they must, their fellow expatriates and they band together for mutual defense and/or offense if aggression should prove to be their best possible defense. In all of this the city itself is nothing more than a continually changing and receptive container. There was never, nor is there, any more than a very transitory line of thought or of conduct in the affairs of the city. It remains an essentially reactive culture, the model of western civilization, the locus of western democratic ideals. Indeed, today, one does not, if one is a white, middle-class educated citizen, come to the city in the spirit of finding a place in a pre-recognized system, so much as one comes with a desire to beat the system (to destroy it) in order to establish a power basis. This is often a prelude to moving on to other worlds to conquer for the young man or woman on the make. In western society, which is in a constant state of fibrillation, the city is seen mainly as an opportunity to capture stray patterns of power, and to bind them together into an oriented, coherent force for personal advancement. There is a strong belief in western society, that the city is a place where one can make good on merit alone, by sheer force of imagination and intellect. This may have been true in the recent past for intellectuals and artists and is therefore assumed to be true in the present, for all. It remains to be proved however, that such a situation obtains for more than a miniscule part of the citizenry. For most the city remains an indifferent or hostile milieu, continually changing but not necessarily for the better, in individual terms. Hence the banding together of the Savoyards or the Auvergnats. The city itself is not a club which one joins, a society for mutual advantage established on clear-cut premises, a hierarchy to ascend or a benevolent protective organization in which to shelter; although it may be all or any of these for certain favored groups.

The city is then, essentially, a fairly fertile terrain to till for those whose ambition (or greed) drives them from their ancestral domains. While the greatness of the 'great cities' may be traced to their emergence as colonial states, the cities themselves were seen as new lands – in a sense, colonies – to conquer by some members of the rural, colonized population. As soon as this counter-movement against the cities began there came into being (under the guise of enlightened city planning) a host of rules and regulations to protect the (established) citizen, and these generally took the form of zoning resolutions to keep out, or at least restrict, undesirables. In the light of what we think we know today, most of these rules and regulations appear as not only anti-democratic but also anti-urban. By the time these rules to exclude or control people came into use, the great cities were rapidly losing their aura of greatness and sliding, greased with the lubricant of colonialism, and the graphite of anti-colonialism, into a micro-cosmic reflection of the aristocratic–feudal world which, in their greatness, they had temporarily eluded.

We have inherited these cities, whose ancient structures are overlaid with modern expedients. They have, in most cases, continued to grow in both population and area, and that growth has usually occurred haphazardly, sometimes almost clandestinely. The result has been urban chaos and suburban sprawl, both of which produce effects far more oppressive, in all likelihood, than any experienced under past tyrannies. The ideal of an open society, a classless political organism, has not given rise to an urbanism or an architecture of cities which could be considered commensurate with its spiritual worth. The result may lead us to question the application of that high ideal.

To most of us in western cities, it appears that the ideal of participatory decision-making has either never been practised or has withered in the climate of exclusionary politicking; i.e. it has never really achieved any credence. The open society, the classless political organism, would surely have produced a more compatible urban environment than that which we presently suffer. It is obvious for instance, that not all urban areas are equal. The sixteenth *arrondissement* of Paris is another country, different in every way from the twelfth or the twentieth. Even in the leveling geometry of the New York grid there is no comparison, in environmental impact, between Manhattan's fashionable East Side and East Harlem. We've clearly been unable to create and maintain even a minimum standard of environment decency across any of our western cities. The fault, of course, lies not in the plan but in ourselves. In fact generally, in northern and western countries we do not practice democracy, nor

do we live in an open society, but rather we hold these up as ideals to be revered, while going about the sordid business of getting and spending; a business which seems to rely entirely upon economic or financial oppression of one class by another. It may well be that the physical disorders which trouble our cities are, after all, an accurate representation of the moral disorders which trouble our society. There is no clear idea or image of society in any of the countries of the capitalist northern hemisphere and it is hard to judge how clear the idea might be in socialist countries. If the architecture of a culture may be said, like any other art, to illuminate that culture, then the outlook for our future is dismal indeed as it appears under the light which is shed by current examples of city building. We seem to be lost in a welter of conflicting ambitions and desires, goals and aims, needs and aspirations. The city now appears more often as a great battlefield, than a place of cooperation and exchange. Neighborhoods and communities, classes, races, sexes and ages are set one against the other, each striving to obtain power, which means power over the others, to impose its own set of rules as the law of the city. The idea of the city as a place which can and should accommodate variety is in the process of disappearing. The city becomes more and more a juxtaposition of incompatible entities, or would-be entities. These disparate pieces are not however, self-sufficient. They are still inter-dependent for almost all of their material needs, such as infra-structure, administration and distribution systems. They need to cohabit because it is the city itself – the center of a web of exchange of goods and services – which is their reason for being. Only a fool

4. *We have inherited those cities, whose ancient structures are overlaid with modern expedients. They have, in most cases, continued to grow in both population and area, and that growth has usually occurred haphazardly, sometimes almost clandestinely. The result has been urban chaos and suburban sprawl ...* View of Paris – Asnières.

5. *The city now appears more often as a great battlefield, rather than a place of cooperation and exchange.* Paris, May 1968. Demonstrators throwing paving blocks.

would choose to live in a western city today, were it not absolutely essential to his material and spiritual existence.

Perhaps the very notion of living in a western city is foolish. Earlier reference was made to Fourier and to his ideas, later appropriated by Marx and Lenin, and currently adopted in some socialist countries. The city in which we live is the antithesis of those ideas. And yet it is ours, sometimes by inheritance, often by our own volition. In exercising our will, in choosing to live in the unliveable city, we appropriate it. Why do we do this? We choose the city because it is absolutely essential to our material and spiritual existence. We may ask ourselves, 'Where else, in spite of everything, could we live?' I would argue that nowhere but in the city can the urban deviate's daily diet be provided. First of all: food and shelter. When people are thrown off the land, as they have been, consistently, over the past half-century, where can they go for food and shelter if not to the city; the center of decisions which affect their access to vital necessities? Rural disintegration, under the pressure of agricultural efficiency, leads to urban compaction as the pressure builds. People who are thrown off the land, in the name of agricultural efficiency, have no recourse but the city where, fortunately, social consciousness has prevailed. The city provides; and first of all it provides food and shelter. It cannot fail to provide these; if it did it would cease to exist as an essential part of the twentieth-century transformation from a rural to an urban economy. The city may be thought of as the graveyard where our economic mistakes will be buried, or as the hospital where they might be cured (or at least, treated). If we refer to the city as a place which at least provides food and shelter, that may appear strange, but it is, in fact, the only place which may be relied upon to provide those essentials, once the rural society and its economy have been destroyed and rebuilt on principles of management. This reliance upon the city as the provider of last resort may be temporary; let us hope that it will be. None the less, for the uprooted peasant, the city is his only resort.

The city also provides an identity, however seemingly fragmented, for its citizens, however recent. It is, to be sure, an identity of a special kind. The city has been, over recent years, a collection point for the people who have been forced, in one way or another, out of their tribal or feudal associations, cast adrift. When people come to the city they begin (and they continue) to identify with it. Since there is, in our society, nowhere else for the outcasts of our economic system to find a home base, it seems clear that many new citizens will embrace the city, perhaps for reasons of expedience, but then, what else could they do? So they appropriate an inherited urban complex (in every sense of the word) and they establish an urban identity. They know where they are, they know who they are (Savoyards or Auvergnats).

No matter who they are, they have become full citizens, and they are fully aware of the strange world in which they live. This acceptance and awareness is of course only natural, in abstract terms, but in reality it represents a considerable reshaping of attitudes.

The more fortunate, or more aware, among them seize upon the city, map out their own constellations of activities within it, live it thoroughly and sometimes even grow to love it, as it becomes theirs. The less fortunate, probably the majority, can yet see the city as a place to be themselves. They can, if they wish, experience the almost-anonymous support of their society. It may only seem to them a place in which one cannot either starve or freeze to death. This may indeed be cold comfort for the displaced, but the city at least provides a place for them to go to when the places from which they come have rejected them.

Perhaps the motives for the movement of young men and women toward the cities are not only ambition or greed but simple necessity. The countryside will no longer support them and their newly-discovered need for a better life. They are conditioned, through the all-pervasive channels of communications systems, to aspire to a more active level of consumption of goods. It is only natural then that they should seek to fulfill those needs, in the only way which is open to them, that is, through emigration from their hamlets and villages and through immigration to the urban centers of the labor market. In a sense, they are on a sinking ship and their only hope is to throw themselves overboard, into the life-giving sea of urban development, however chaotic that may seem. Thus the city, with all its hardships, may seem more hospitable than the countryside, with all its implacable constraints. The city seems at least permeable and malleable; the countryside holds no hope, save for a few, who are strong enough and shrewd enough to grasp its essential force, which is autocratic and based upon the idea of the survival of the fittest, and the reality cf mechanized agriculture which leads to a devaluation of agricultural labor. As new 'needs' are implanted in the rural population, new techniques reduce the returns which a man might expect from his efforts on the land. As industry rises, agriculture declines. Men no longer produce, or expect to produce, sustenance for their fellow man in the same ratios of effort and time which held true over the past generations. Agriculture itself has become an industry, and one which accounts for less than one tenth of the total effort required to fuel the current economy. It is not startling then that we should say that the city (which controls the remaining 90 per cent of production) remains the only hope for persons displaced by these powerful changes.

For most of them, the city has become the place which provides, or can provide warmth, food and possibly love. The warmth may be animal or spiritual; the food may be as much for the mind as for the stomach; the love may vary with the vagaries of human association. The fact is that there is no warmth, food or love left in the depleted countryside, transformed by agri-business into an exclusive domain. There is nowhere but the city. The city however is not simply a collection of miserable refugees from the country. At the same time that the country was becoming managed and corporatized the city was becoming a power over that management. Indeed the corporatization of the country concentrated more power in the city.

6. *They need to cohabit because it is the city itself – the center of a web of exchange of goods and services – which is their reason for being.* Central markets in Paris – before their removal to the periphery in 1969.

7. *The city provides an identity for its citizens . . . the more fortunate among them seize upon the city, map out their own constellations of activities within it, and often grow to love it as it becomes theirs.* Paris, The Canal St Martin.

The common denominator of city dwellers has become, by the force of movement, their interest in each other. The city is new, in a sense, in our century. The power of urbanization, which accompanied deruralization, has put us all in the same boat. We have a sense of common misfortune, no matter that the boat we are all in often resembles that ill-fated *Radeau de la Méduse*. (The raft from the ship *Méduse* became a chamber of horrors when the good ship sank off the coast of Africa, and almost within sight of it. See, for instance, the famous painting by Géricault. The example is only used to try to illuminate our current situation in which we are all somehow cast adrift. The bark of virtuous effort has foundered under us in the stormy sea of personal gain depersonalized, and we may, if no one climbs the mast to spy out the close-lying land, all perish in an orgy of self-willed, witless cannibalism, even as the castaways of the *Méduse*.) However, recent urban disasters (such as the New York power failure of 1965) need only be researched superficially to convince us that a common misfortune will wipe away most dog-eat-dog attitudes among the new urban population. This seems to indicate that new and old urban populations retain a sense of social responsibility toward each other and themselves. When disaster strikes, the urban forces coalesce: in the absence of disaster they tend to curdle.

Some of us need the city, especially the elders. Children can, of course, adapt to any place and will probably be happiest (for a spell) in the permissive spaces of the suburbs. Artists are content to move to exurbia once they have gotten a start in the city and learned the rules of the games that art dealers play. But most of us need the sense of nearness, of human relationships under the stress of propinquity, of something (good or bad) always happening. The city is not simply a shopping center mall, with programmed activities: people live in it and die in it. It appears that the city is the only viable mass organization which we have been able to produce over centuries of striving to live together.

This does not, to be sure, mean that we are, or should be, quite content with the cities which we have. The citizens will always hope and struggle for improvements in the urban environment. We are not so foolish as to love the city for its faults. We may choose to live with the faults, hoping always to correct them, or to minimize them, but we live with the potential for good and for harmony which we know is in the city. We live, then, in a city of hope, which we know to be the most abiding city of all, and perhaps the only attainable city left to us.

Our city of hope cannot be demonstrated, as a model city should, as for instance the city of the future was, in the General Electric (or was it General Motors?) cyclorama at the Flushing Meadows Fair in 1939. It remains extraordinarily elusive, even today, for it has no corporate funders: it's ours, not theirs. But the abiding city of hope is the city in which every black or chicano, or Puerto-Rican, or West Indian, or Pakistani lives, when he comes to live with us, near the center of the empire. He, or she, can describe it, and if we cannot, then that is a measure of our own Anglo-Saxon shortcomings. Yet, we may say, we made these cities and we should be able to describe their fullness and their emptiness. Not so; we made them but we also lost them in a corrupt game of obviously marked cards. Their evolution, in North America at least, has little to do with our concerns for justice and civic morality. In the face of immoral capitalistic exploitation, our civic morality counts for little. When so much misery is concentrated on so few acres (Notting Hill, Harlem, la Goutte d'Or) justice becomes a different force. We must then speak otherwise, or remain decently silent. However, it is not in our bones to remain silent, and so we would choose to cry out against the indecency of misery concentrated in Notting Hill, la Goutte d'Or, or Harlem. Although we made the cities, we certainly never intended them to reflect so accurately the shortcomings of our society.

Most of the problems which we evoke when we discuss the situation of cities today are problems of growth and change. As long as cities were small, and relatively stable in population, the problems with which we are now concerned were not in evidence. There were other problems, and it would be foolish to regret those old days which were not good for everyone, or even for most people. However we are concerned today with realizing to the fullest the great potential which lies in recently developed political systems which profess openness and brotherhood. The chaotic state of urban development and deterioration today cannot be attributed solely to the move toward popular participatory democracy. It is more probably a natural result of pressures which have been generated by the changes, many of which are in a real sense advances, made in our economic and social conditions over the past few generations. The roots of our present problems cannot all be isolated with any authority. However, we may say that population, increasing at an accelerated rate (the *population bomb*), is certainly part of it. So is the shift from predominantly rural, agricultural activity to urban, industrial production. The idea of wealth as a commodity, with its concomitant notion of extraterritorial expansion of economic activity (*imperi-*

"THAT'S NOT A PLANET — IT'S AN INCUBATOR."

alism) is a contributing factor. All of these provoke profound and continuing stresses in the social structure. All of them, despite their bad press, have been associated with the expression of a need to provide a place for each member of society, where he can participate in its life. That place, probably for reasons of expediency, has for most been the city. The city was the only social and physical structure available on which to build the new world, which still is seen optimistically as a totally open and totally integrated association of free individuals. The chances of building new structures to organize the new world remain entire, and recent developments such as the latest census in the United States indicate that it may be possible to inhibit the growth of cities, although to do this in an orderly and

8. *The roots of our present problems cannot all be isolated with any authority. However, we may say that population, increasing at an accelerated rate (the population bomb), is certainly part of it.* Bill Mauldin, cartoon in the *Chicago Sunday Times*.

9. *So is the shift from predominantly rural, agricultural activity to urban, industrial production.* Lyon, lunch-time at the Berliet factory.

socially profitable way calls for a degree of national and continental planning, which would at present seem to be at considerable variance with western ideologies.

The most recent US census (1970) seems to show a stabilization of city population, as compared to urban population. The statistic is questionable, since for the census-takers cities do not exist. They deal in Standard Metropolitan Statistical Areas and other abstractions which have little to do with the city-dweller's city. However, they show that cities (referred to in the report as inner-cities) have been losing population to suburbs (outer-cities) over the last two decades. This could be heartening news for the city dweller, if it means that the size of the city itself (inner-city) is somehow self-limiting. It may, however, be bad news if it means that the city is really growing but the Feds (the national government) are not only refusing to recognize the fact, but even attempt to bury it statistically.

Such an approach to the handling of intrinsically innocuous statistics would betray an intent on the part of the US government which bodes ill for cities, since the statistics are used for purposes of appropriation of funds. Cheating at such a fundamental level would mean that the city dwellers (citizens) would be cheated at every level. That would indeed be a strange way to operate a democracy. The cities would then become, in fact, colonies of their own country, with outflow of wealth exceeding return. One hesitates to believe that the books could be cooked so outrageously.

We must then assume that the census tells the truth, and that cities in North America are indeed losing population. This would mean that it is possible, however inadvertently, to limit the population of cities. The twentieth-century dream of inhibiting the growth of cities has come to pass, without specific constraints imposed from above. Man, in his essential rightness, has overcome another impossible obstacle and realized another impossible dream. Cities are stabilized. They now only lose (relatively) rich population and gain only (relatively) poor population.

Another phenomenon is demonstrated by the 1970 US census. Cities are becoming more black. In fact people who move out of the 'inner city' are generally white, while people who move in are generally black or brown. Although this does not concur with the American dream of an egalitarian society, the facts cannot be denied: American cities are becoming darker as well as poorer.

One may dispute the census findings on grounds of interpretation, but not on statistical grounds. The statistics are, of course, inaccurate but they may be said to be a close approximation as the errors tend to cancel out. (Black leaders estimate that about 10 to 20 per cent of the black population is not counted at all, and is thus disenfranchised.) On the grounds of interpretation we may say that cities in the broader sense of metropolitan areas dependent upon cities are in fact gaining population. Cities are growing and expanding in low-density patterns. More and more people are living, if not in the cities, at least off the cities. No one is returning to the land; the cities are growing and spreading. The movement of population is still immigration to the city and emigration from the center to the edge of the city. The census is telling us that we have not achieved stability in urban growth but that we have changed the population in the center, with a slight loss in numbers, while increasing the total number of people who are using the city.

Even if growth, scatter and sprawl could, theoretically, be limited at the expense of free choice, change itself will not, and cannot, be contained by the fiat of planners. Change in centuries past was often imperceptible. It now occurs at an accelerated, and still accelerating, rate of speed. Cities, by virtue of their complex and continuous demands for a variety of services, many of which must be built-in in order to operate effectively, are generally resistant to change. In their initial growth periods they do change rapidly, and tend toward increased efficiency. The change which accompanies growth becomes more and more difficult to achieve as the mass of buildings becomes ever greater. Significant changes in the physical composition of the city, or even in its multiple functions, are increasingly hard to make as investments accumulate. In spite of the difficulties however, the essential fact of urban life today is change. When it cannot take place within an existing order, it takes place without order, in apparent disorder.

But these words are misleading, for change is an order in itself: the

10. *In spite of the difficulties however, the essential fact of urban life today is change. When it cannot take place within an existing order, it takes place without order, in apparent disorder.* Boston 'Government Center'.

11. *Now since change is the natural order, one of the essential goals of architecture and urbanism is to conceive of structures which will make the city more adaptable to necessary and ineluctable changes in function, and in the relationships between functions, which must continue to occur.* Model of structuring system proposed for Frankfurt city center 1961. (Architects: Candilis, Josic, Woods and Schiedhelm.) A multi-layered web of pedestrian ways serving a variety of uses. See Chap. 2, pp. 123 ff.

natural order of all things. If a city is unresponsive to, or incapable of accommodating change, a chaotic unruly state will prevail. Now since change is the natural order, one of the essential goals of architecture and urbanism is to conceive of structures which will make the city more adaptable to necessary and ineluctable changes in function, and in the relationships between functions, which must continue to occur.

These essential goals of architecture and urbanism today are not very different from those of the past. But our societies are very different, and we are concerned with making places and organizing ways within which our new societies can function easily and correctly. We use the plural because we do not see one ideal society, but rather a number of societies in a state of becoming. We can no longer conceive, as our enlightened ancestors could, an ideal society in an ideal city. And this is because the time dimension has become as important to us as the other three dimensions of space. Our ideal cannot exist, even in an ideal state, for we have many ideals and the

urban structures which we propose to realize will need to accommodate all or most of them (as well as the unimagined ideals which might be formulated by our immediate successors) if they are to prove viable.

A principal goal of urbanism is to correspond to the needs of people who are its first concern. We contend that the planning and building, and the replanning and rebuilding of our environment is directed toward making it as responsive as possible to the expression of the goals of the people, whose life support it is. The complex of cities and towns, of villages and farms, which makes up our social and physical environment exists only in order to sustain the bodies and minds of the citizens, and they are therefore most concerned in the sweet workings of the system.

12. *However, the man in the street, the anonymous statistic of history, has in our time divided and multiplied, like an amoeba, except that in his many manifestations he is not entirely a predictable carbon copy of the original. Certainly, he never was entirely predictable, and statistical analysis was probably always a poor substitute for the vastly unpredictable diversity of human fact. The man in the street, and the man in the field or forest, are demonstrably many.* Paris, rue de Buci. Klebphoto by Vera Spoerri.

However, the man in the street, the anonymous statistic of history, has in our time divided and multiplied, like an amoeba except that in his many manifestations he is not entirely a predictable carbon copy of the original. Certainly he never was entirely predictable, and statistical analysis was probably always a poor substitute for the vastly unpredictable diversity of human fact. The man in the street, and the man in the field or forest, are demonstrably many. Our political systems may seek always to reduce to a minimum the diverse qualities of their constituencies, but the system, or the city, which does not accommodate diversity is inevitably repressive. The man is many: he has many occupations and preoccupations, he speaks with many tongues and holds to many ideals. An urbanism which concerns him will need to accommodate itself to the diverse

truths of his conflicting needs, desires, ambitions, motivations, passions and indifferences, for there is no simple truth which fits him. He is not a statistical manikin, on rails as it were, thoroughly programmed and efficiently channeled to desire and to aspire to everything that the urban theorist decrees to be desirable, or what the theorist's own programming allows him to perceive as being desirable. Urbanism is not a polemic but neither is it an argument for the attainment of a presumably desirable urban state of being – a golden age. We should remember that gold is one of the most inert elements (wherein lies its value). A golden age is dormant. Urbanism should rather try to deal with a largely unknown state of becoming. It should be thought of as keeping all the options for as long a time as possible.

To do this, to keep options open, urbanism itself must be adaptable to change. An urbanism of change, one that takes the fact of inevitable change as one of its components, can perhaps include all the options. It can at least encompass many of them. We refer principally to political options, to those systems which control and convey the power to allocate the resources of the world, and to decide how they will be used. Systems may be open or closed, and that which is open can later be closed and controlled as the need arises, should the need arise. A closed system cannot be opened; it can only be destroyed. An urbanism of change would be able to accommodate all the choices, even including stability, or resistance to change. An urbanism of constancy, or composition, based upon an ideal system, cannot allow for change, since change is its enemy, indeed its destruction.

Urbanism then should be seen as a radical, progressive discipline, as open and unconstrained as possible. Only from such a standpoint can all the rich and diverse forces which are present in society continually be productive and a place be made, equitably, for all. The urbanism of change, radical progressive urbanism, can contain many visions of the city, because it is organic and dynamic in its intentions. It responds to life and to changing social, economic and political conditions. The urbanism of constancy, of spatial composition, can tolerate no vision but its own dead stereotype of an ideal state.

Urbanism is the ordering of the built world, which is to say practically all of our world. This is especially true for the industrialized countries of Europe and America. Those other countries which are so fortunate as to retain a tribal or religious tradition will have no use, or very little use, for this treatise. They have, first of all, no need to even think about urbanism. No part of their habitat can so easily be separated from the rest. One could say that life is urbanism, for instance, and so saying one would be envious. There could never be considered an urbanism which would be other than traditional and life-supporting. We, however, have managed to divorce the idea of urbanism, of physical planning, from our life styles. It has become something apart, something even less than politics. We have, God help us, invented the urbanist, who must rule our routes and sewers and let us live together in the promiscuity of common drains. We have urbanists, we have urbanism, because we have chosen to live together, and thus our world has become a totally built world, entirely constructed with our own wills. This is what our industry has led us to: we need someone (one of us) to tell us what to build, and where and when to build it. We do not feel the need for someone to tell us why we need build whatever it is that we build. We feel we know that instinctively.

Urbanism is the ordering of the built world, which is the natural (some would say unnatural) habitat of man. The built world is most highly concentrated in cities which are made up of a range of places, from public to private, along with a complex of distribution and servicing systems designed to enable certain activities to be carried out in those places.

The idea of city as a place for exchange but also as a place for all of life implies that there is more to it than just a collection of places, all plugged in to adequate systems of support. Men come to cities also to find the support of society, the apparent safety of numbers (in which perhaps there is no safety), the company of miserable peers. When life on the land is decreed to be no longer possible for more than 5 to 10 per cent of the population – agriculture's share of the national product – the move to the city is forced upon those whom rural activities will no longer support. Usually the city is unprepared, or ill-prepared to receive the influx of excess rural population. The

13. *The idea of city as a place for exchange but also as a place for all of life implies that there is more to it than just a collection of places, all plugged in to adequate systems of support.* (above) Paris, Vert Galant garden, at Pont Neuf.

14. *The move to the city is forced upon those whom rural activities will no longer support. Usually the city is unprepared or ill-prepared to receive an influx of excess rural population. The migration is disorganized, spontaneous, obeying undisclosed laws. The resulting urban growth is chaotic and characterized by congestion and lack of supporting services.* (top right) Paris, Bidonville at Nanterre.

15. *Congestion, of course, engenders conflict, and 'safety in numbers' becomes the terror of numbers.* (right) Paris, traffic jammed.

migration is disorganized, spontaneous, obeying undisclosed laws. The resulting urban growth is chaotic and characterized by congestion and lack of all the supporting services; as well as lack of living space. Congestion, of course, engenders conflict, and 'safety in numbers' becomes the terror of numbers.

This situation leads one to imagine that there is another way to consider the built world – not as city and country in mutual opposition, but as parts of a single operating entity. Then urbanism, the concern for man's natural habitat, must be preoccupied with not only the city but with the entire regional, national or continental context. A country or continent might be considered a great city with vast open spaces in it. A city must be taken in its regional context; it includes vast open spaces and virtually all man's activities and tranquillities. The interdependence of urban and rural economies is obvious. It remains for us to integrate them spatially and politically into one functioning organism, each giving and receiving support from the other. Communications have made bedfellows of urban and rural populations, and they need not be strange to one another. In today's world an inordinate strain is placed on both urban and rural populations when they are considered separately, as distinct, detachable or compartmented species. This is not only economic nonsense, leading to the widely-held view that each is a colony of the other, but it generates artificial human conflicts with bitter animosity and waste at the absurd end of this witless logic. City mouse and country mouse are both, after all, mice. Both may profit from their common mousehood.

1. Urbanism and Urban Evolution

As the world changes, cities evolve, and expand or perhaps die. Urbanism is the activity of society which concerns itself with the direction of that evolution with a view toward controlling it for the greatest benefit of the greater number. The energy released by evolutionary change in cities and countries of the west could be seen as a force which can be recovered and used to further the goals of society, as society understands them. The agglomeration of farms, for instance, into units of greater apparent economic strength releases an enormous potential in manpower. Farmers and agricultural workers, no longer effectively employed at rural pursuits, are switched to the industrial or service labor market.

This transference of the worker, the unit of production, from one kind of activity to another, creates not only a quantum of energy but also a host of problems of dislocation and relocation, of habitat and infrastructure. In a similar way, the growth of service industries and other essentially non-productive occupations, the vast expansion of administration and government in all of the western countries, creates new strains and stresses in the urban industrial complex. The increase in absolute population, although not as dramatic in the western part of the northern hemisphere as it is on the rest of the globe, also imposes new constraints on the context of urban evolution. These forces at work will not be, and should not be, considered as either positive or negative in their ultimate effect on human habitat but, more reasonably, as changing parts of the environment, which, for most of us, is the built world.

Generally, in the milieu with which we are concerned, the growth of cities, or urbanized regions, is taken for granted. The advent of specialized mass production, the industrial revolution, seems to have cut us off forever from the bucolic purviews and pursuits of our ancestors. It may not be true that all progress is good. Indeed, it may rightfully be questioned that urban man today is better off than his rural ancestors. However, it appears that most of us are committed, willy-nilly, to the urban adventure, the collective destiny, and this being the case we would do well to take a cold-eyed look at what sort of environment we can establish for ourselves and for our children, in our parishes and on our globe.

In the last century or so, we have seen enormous growth in size, population and wealth of our ancient cities, once the abode of princes and the centers of exchange for what were essentially agricultural products. Urbanization, in modern history, has been an accelerating process with each new wave of immigration adding to the potential for further growth. Once the safety-valve of external colonialism ceased to function, through the exportation of even more sophisticated and effective techniques of preserving health and disseminating knowledge, the home cities of the colonialists entered into a period of crisis. This crisis, which is today acute in most of the self-styled 'developed countries,' manifests itself generally in the ways which are confusing to the citizens, however clear they may seem to historians, economists and other persons who have acquired the skill of detaching themselves from their immediate surroundings and constraints.

'Great cities' (the very term is a résumé of colonialism) are seen to be, increasingly, in great financial and social difficulties. They cannot only exist as the preserves and playgrounds of capitalist entrepreneurs, for those rapacious captains are no longer prepared, or competent, to sustain the center of their activities They invented, or re-invented the city (or more simply recognized it as the best possible locus of their moneymaking), but they, and we, now see that the city is no longer manageable at their scale.

The city has taken on a life of its own, it obeys other laws than the first law of motion or the law of supply and demand. One wonders whether the urbanization process is irreversible. Will a new form of internal colonialism again shift populations, from the cities to another locus of exploitation and moneymaking? It is difficult to imagine such a future situation. Where and how would it be? One feels that such speculation is footling (and that its prevalence in western journalism is more a case of distractive tactics than a genuine cause for alarm) in view of the vast and pressing problems which confront us today. The future promises virtually no haven from present problems, and provides, at best, an extraordinarily precarious perch. We would be better occupied with our present dilemma, than with essentially idle speculations about future solutions.

There has been much talk, in such respected places as the *New York Times*, for instance, about the new American city, which when described turns out to be the old American suburb, motorized and shopping-centered. This is said to be the wave, and the way of the future: scattered low-density development spotted here and there with commercial oases, scaled to the wasteful speed of the motor car, uniform in every way possible, from financial to political and ethical attitudes, a politician's paradise of quiescent, complacent consumers.

Other scenarios depict a future of exotic technologies (and doubtless many of these will eventually become reality) operating within mythical organizations of science-fiction structures; soaring cities for superman. We are promised climate control, and virtually every other conceivable kind of control, some of which appear as less than desirable.

Unfortunately most futuristic visions of urban life and form do not include any provision for recovery and conversion of the existing built domain, which represents the major investment of materials and labor since the world began. Such massive investment can hardly be simply ignored or discarded. In any urban future the urban past will play the major role. In this sense the only possible future lies in the past, i.e. in the re-use or continued use of existing investments in construction and equipment. Given time to think, how ridiculous it is to envisage a London without Tubes, a Paris without the Métro! The history of urbanism can be seen to parallel the myth of the phoenix, and nothing will be born if the ashes of the past are recklessly scattered. Admittedly the Tubes and the Métro are in sorry state; they need renovation. But one cannot envision, rationally, their being

16. *Urbanization in modern history has been an accelerating process with each new wave of immigration adding to the potential for further growth.* (below) Population distribution in the Paris area.

17. *One wonders whether the urbanization process is irreversible. Will a new form of internal colonialism again shift populations, from the cities to another locus of exploitation and moneymaking?* (right) Levittown, New York.

18. *Unfortunately most futuristic visions of urban life and form do not include any provision for recovery and conversion of the existing built domain, which represents the major investment of materials and labor since the world began. Such massive investment can hardly be simply ignored or discarded. In any urban future the urban past will play the major role.* (below right) Paris, excavation for parking garage under the Parvis Notre Dame. Archaeological remains of Lutetia were, of course, uncovered.

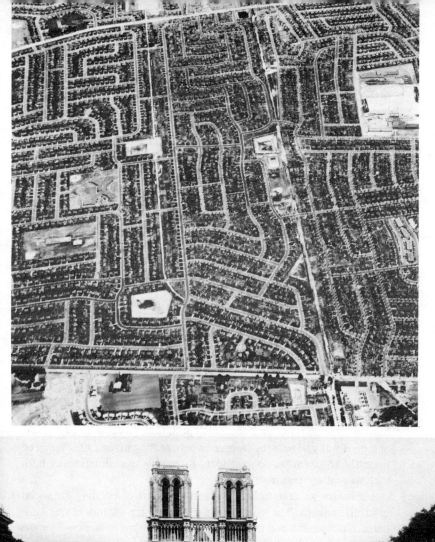

tied-off, or plugged-up, to favor new, largely untried, systems of transport. In a similar vein, although the moonshots have proved man's ability to live, to a degree, upon his own biological resources, through technologically sophisticated systems of recovery and purification, the demonstration does not indicate any feasible end to sewage treatment and water supply systems as we know them. The spaceship concept is a vast, global one, and does not prove out at the individual level, principally because it would require an enormous expenditure of energy. Space is vast, and the polluting by-products of great energy expenditures can be (for the moment) swallowed in it. The world is small, and shrinking; any extra energy-producing burden translates immediately into ambient pollution.

We had best leave these high energy consuming visions to the journalists, whose view is limited to their local experience, and consider rather how to cope, in a realistic way, with our present dilemma.

Our dilemma is real. In practically all of the cities of the west we are faced with problems of expansion, congestion, renewal and growth. These problems are demographic, economic, social, political and, more to the point, human. The 'great cities' and countries of the west live today in inconceivable, but real, squalor. Urban poverty, human degradation, environmental pollution, psychic stress, crime and civil war are now the normal events of the citizen's life. We need urgently to examine, to consider, to rectify our situation as both victims and oppressors.

Urbanism we take to be the science and art of building for social interrelationship. The village or the hamlet are no longer our concern. We have escaped them, for good, or bad, but in any case for the present. The suburbs of Scandinavia, England or America are sources of concern, in a sense, expressions of imminent atomic warfare, the latest development in the citizen's continuing war against himself; the latest formulation of the 'I'm all right Jack' philosophy: colonialism on a quarter-acre scale.

But our real concern is in the cities, in their deterioration, their seeming hopelessness. For cities are, after all, the focal points of virtually all social and cultural endeavor as well as being nodes on

19. *The 'great cities' and countries of the west live today in inconceivable squalor.* Scene in Watts section of Los Angeles after 1965 riots.

20. *Urban poverty, human degradation, environmental pollution, psychic stress, crime and civil war are now the normal events of the citizen's life.* Venice, canal pollution.

21. *Urbanism we take to be the science and art of building for social interrelationship. The village or the hamlet are no longer our concern. We have escaped them, for good, or bad, but in any case for the present. The suburbs of Scandinavia, England and America are sources of concern* ... (below) Wilmington, California, view of an American suburb.

22. *Our civilization, whatever we may think of it, is urban, at least for the present.* (right) Lyon, arcade.

23. *All the cities of the west, from Stockholm to Naples and from Leningrad to Los Angeles, have some more or less magnificent relics to the conscience of their exploiters.* (below right) Milan, Galleria Vittorio Emanuele II. A magnificent and useful piece of urban design.

the financial network. They are still the seats of government (with its expanding bureaucracy) and power. The decisions which count for the present and future of western society are still made in, and colored by, cities. Judging from the American example, where the focus of power has shifted from the rural, feudal, landed élite, to the suburbs, one might venture, were one trendy, to say that future power centers will be in the cities which are the centers of those suburbs. Our civilization, whatever we may think of it, is urban, at least for the present. That is why we are here concerned essentially with cities and their possibilities of evolution in terms of urbanism, which is everybody's architecture.

Urbanism is a relatively new field of study. In the good/bad old days of free enterprise, free market capitalism, urbanism was left to the conscience of the rich. What needed to be done was done, or not, but it was only done either as what we now recognize as a salve to a guilty, bleeding conscience or as a stimulant to a lagging market. All of the cities of the west, from Stockholm to Naples, and from Leningrad to Los Angeles, have some more or less magnificent relics to the conscience of their exploiters. But today, it doesn't pay, or is no longer fashionable to be both fortuned and conscientious.

Cities and the people in them are left to their own meager devices while their resources (by way of taxes) go into rocketry and atomic bluff, defense of the 'state,' prestige, glamour, and old-fashioned boondoggling in the form of intra- and inter-continental super-highways, moonshots, real-estate promotion and other good works. We are told that an expanding 'national product' will take care of our problems, and yet the gap between rich and poor grows ever wider, both locally and globally.

The Essential Goals of Urbanism

It is undoubtedly pretentious for the urbanist to aspire to the correction of social ills through the application of design and programming skills, and imagination, to the physical planning of the urban environment. 'We shape our buildings and are formed by them,' as Churchill said, is only part of the story. We work within a given social, economic and political context and our designs are necessarily conditioned by those systems. Indeed, our designs reveal more tellingly than any written critique the nature of the systems and their shortcomings. In this sense urbanists might be called revolutionaries, or at least agents-provocateurs, for their actions and inactions give substance and urgency to the inequities of the institutional arrangements which govern the lives of the urban masses. Decisions and indecisions at the level of government translate into built form: transportation systems, buildings, etc. Responsibility is placed upon the urbanists who only execute those decisions or are frustrated by those indecisions. In all cases, the inadequacies of present

24. *We work within a given social, economic and political context and our designs are necessarily conditioned by those systems. Indeed, our designs reveal more tellingly than any written critique the nature of the systems and their shortcomings.* Paris, view of new buildings in air-rights of Main-Montparnasse rail station.

25. *Unfortunately, the links between cause and effect are often shrouded in political mysticism or mystification so that immediate remedial action can rarely be obtained. In this area the power of the people is usually dissipated in inconsequential holding actions ... The larger picture, however, is not affected by popular miscontent.* The Los Angeles Freeway – part of a federally-funded national system.

administrative systems, in the evolution of the physical environment, are fully exposed to public view. The built world bears pressing testimony, which cannot be ignored, to the shortcomings of an overwhelmed political and administrative system. The fact that we pretend to the arts and sciences of urbanism only serves to underscore and demonstrate those inadequacies to the citizens who are alert enough to relate cause and effect in the urban disaster which has grown out of them. In a homeopathic way, society has secreted a cure (at least for some of the symptoms) in its own illness. However homeopathy may be of little use to the victims of an accident of the magnitude which has befallen our cities and our society.

Unfortunately, the links between cause and effect are often shrouded in political mysticism and mystification so that immediate remedial action can rarely be obtained. In this area, the power of the people is usually dissipated in inconsequential holding actions which seek to contain (and sometimes succeed in turning back) the most flagrant instances of urbanistic mayhem. The larger picture, however, is not affected by mere popular miscontent, and this is usually because the politicians and their administrations have become so adept at the techniques of misdirection. The practise of urbanism, whether preventive or curative, would require a revision of priorities, a fundamental change in the use of a country's resources of wealth and energy. However, it is in the nature of bureaucracy to oppose change, and all countries of the west are afflicted with increasing bureaucratic sclerosis. Even reformist administrations begin by creating new agencies which do not replace, but only extend the old ones, so firmly established that they cannot be dislodged.

Bureaucracy has, of course, a long history of stability, of opposing change. Each agency develops its own concepts on how to oppose change; some do it bluntly and some subtly, but all do it, whence Parkinson's law. Stalin had a radical remedy for the bureaucratic establishment, which consisted of removing the bureau chiefs periodically and often violently. One is not prepared to condemn him out of hand for these so-called excesses, which at least may have had the virtue of providing a model for the permanent cultural revolution of Chairman Mao.

26. *The practise of urbanism, whether preventive or curative, would require a revision of priorities, a fundamental change in the use of a country's resources of wealth and energy.* A young campaigner in the 1970 Greater London Council elections, where some saw the issue as being reduced to a choice between roads and homes. This was, according to the *Observer*, the first time in England that a consumer group had tried to accede to political power through the political process. They lost, this time.

In the west, we tend to conserve the established bureaucracies (it is politic to do so) and to establish new ones to perform the same function. Whether this is reform of the administrative system or simply redirection of graft is never quite clear. We are accustomed to graft as a way of administration and tend not to question too closely the recipients. Why should we? Rather than fight bureaucratic bribe-taking, we prefer to pretend that it does not, and could not, exist. Nonetheless we know that it does exist, and that each expansion of the bureaucracy means a redistribution of the spoils of political victory. And, of course, we realize that the spoils are ours to give, to the politicos which we currently favor. We have, however, in spite of this political sophistication, very little concept of the relationship between political expediency and urbanistic policy.

Urbanism aims to direct and control the physical environment for the greater good of the greatest number. It seeks to do this through planning, programming and design of the built world. The goals of urbanism are relatively simple to enunciate. We might mention, for instance, the distribution of economic, social and cultural activities throughout the urban fabric; the installation of smoothly functioning systems of circulation; the articulation of public and private domains in comprehensible patterns, in ways which reduce, rather than produce, conflict; the efficient and pleasant use of urban space, both built and unbuilt; the ordering of the city's activities and tranquillities in ways that can remain responsive to the citizen's desires and criteria. More specifically, we would say that the city should be not only for the people who live in it but also of them and by them.

The economic base should be decongested and distributed. A Quartier de la Défense (Paris) kind of concentration makes no more sense, in the daily life of the city, than the midtown Manhattan or lower Manhattan office towers, clustering in obedience to fundamentally irrelevant reasons. Those towers at la Défense, as in Manhattan, are full of jobs, but those who work there cannot live there or anywhere near there. It has become commonplace for urbanists to argue for a redistribution of activities over wider areas. However, real estate interests obviously do not agree with this view, and a valid subject of inquiry would be to try to understand why this is so. It seems to have more to do with the tradition of the market-place – a place where the action is – than with a reasoned appreciation of what might work best. In recent years it has become apparent that concentration of 'business' activities in a given area (the 'city') has very little justification in fact. Most 'business' is transacted by wire or mail; there is very little personal contact involved. A simile for the electronic

27. *The goals of urbanism are relatively simple to enunciate. We might mention, for instance, the distribution of economic, social and cultural activities throughout the urban fabric* ... (left) Rue de la Gaite, in the Montparnasse section of Paris, where shops, offices, music-halls and theaters co-exist with dwellings.

28. *The goals of urbanism ... sweetly functioning systems of circulation.* (right) Public and private transportation systems, each with its own path and scale of speed.

29. *The goals of urbanism are relatively simple ... the efficient and pleasant use of urban space, both built and unbuilt.* Venice, the Piazza San Marco.

30. *The goals of urbanism ... the ordering of the city's activities and tranquillities in ways that can remain responsive to the citizen's desires and criteria.* Paris, the Palais Royal, an island of tranquillity bordered by a sea of activity.

way of doing business may be seen in the design of the World Trade Center, in lower Manhattan, where two identical towers reach to preposterous heights, with no inter-connections save by telephone (with duplication of mains some 200 feet apart). It is inconceivable that the bureaucrat on the eightieth floor of the south tower would ever meet face to face with his opposite number on the seventy-second floor of the north tower. Both are plugged in to the same telephone system, and through it have the same access to the same computer which may be located 200 or 3,000 miles away. The only result of their proximity is shared inconvenience in getting to and from their offices, and that is caused by the overloading of an inadequate transportation system. (The underground, the buses and even the pavements will be overcrowded when both buildings are occupied.) The irony of this situation is that the World Trade Center is built by an administration whose role was, and is, to coordinate and improve transportation facilities in the New York Metropolitan area. That administration, the Port of New York Authority, has clearly abandoned its charter. From a planning agency it has evolved to become a real estate speculator. But even so, one is perplexed by the insistence on locating some 9,000,000 additional square feet of office space in lower Manhattan, an area already congested with office workers and not particularly accessible from those workers' homes. Congestion is piled upon confusion.

The same idiocy characterizes the development in the west of Paris, Neuilly and the Quartier de la Défense. If at some time an argument could be made for proximity, in the City of London or around Wall Street when messages were hand-carried, that argument no longer can be said to be convincing. The office-boy – 'runner' – has disappeared. Contemporary means of communication have rendered this kind of proximity obsolete. One may perhaps seek the reasons for continued concentration in other, extraneous concerns, such as habit, prestige, land-speculation and political pressures. There is surely no demonstrable functional or urbanistic reason. On the contrary, the concentration of 9 a.m. to 5 p.m. tertiary activity on a limited acreage, with room for nothing else, can only be seen as non-functional and anti-urbanistic.

31. *The economic base should be decongested and distributed. A Quartier de la Défense kind of concentration of office buildings makes no more sense, in the daily life of the city, than the midtown Manhattan or lower Manhattan office towers, clustering in obedience to fundamentally irrelevant laws. Those towers, at la Défense as in Manhattan, are full of jobs, but those who work there cannot live there, or anywhere near there.* Paris, office towers at la Défense, a new commercial development in the west of Paris, at Neuilly. As Bishop Berkeley once said, 'The march of progress is ever to the west.'

32. *If at some time an argument could be made for proximity . . . contemporary means of communication have rendered proximity obsolete.* American Telephone and Telegraph Company's 'Picturephone' transmitter-receiver.

33. *The creation of education ghettos, at Nanterre or Vincennes, makes no more sense than their existence at Oxbridge or Cambridge, Mass. Those ghettos are full of knowledge but they are removed from the daily life of the city and kept inaccessible to the great numbers who could both benefit from their proximity and contribute to their support.* Up-to-date educational ghetto at Nanterre, where the May 1968 trouble started.

The creation of educational ghettos, at Nanterre or Vincennes, makes no more sense than their existence at Oxbridge, or Cambridge, Mass. Those ghettos are full of knowledge but they are removed from the daily life of the city and kept inaccessible to the great numbers who could both benefit from their proximity and contribute to their support. Educational ghettos are, of course, very functional. The dissociation of life and 'education,' especially 'higher education' has long been seen as a desirable situation. How else could young minds be so easily bent? The ruling élite has always been, since the time of Plato at least, preoccupied with the formation of suitable heritors. The education mystique plays a major role in that formation. While the young are being trained to rule, they must be sheltered from life as it is lived under the rulers. For reason and natural reactions Aristotelian logic must be substituted for language, jargon or dead tongues. The dissemination of knowledge has to be rigidly controlled and the use of knowledge even more so. Indeed, in western universities, the concept of knowledge is that of a rare commodity which needs to be guarded, lest it become common knowledge, accessible to all. Like the diamond it has unquestionable utilitarian value but its price derives from artificially imposed scarcity. To maintain the price the workers must be isolated and closely controlled.

The prestige with which educational facilities – especially those whose thresholds are forbidden to the general public through one device (e.g. cost) or another (e.g. academic requirements) – have surrounded themselves, is a source of perplexity. The City University of New York is a rare example of an organization which is continually evolving toward interdependence with the city itself. Politically, it is in great difficulty. Both faculty and alumni oppose the opening of the University to the people who support it. Opposition is predictably (but unconvincingly) based upon the maintenance of high academic standards. Of what use are academic standards which operate to exclude most of the constituents of the University to the detriment of the general level of education in the city? Exclusive academic standards make nonsense of the entire notion of general (or 'public') education. They are also anti-economic, and in the largest sense, anti-social. Harvard, Yale, Cambridge, Oxford, les Grandes Écoles in France, Heidelberg and *tutti quanti* may or may not be prestigious. They are certainly counter-productive in our society which is supposed to be trying to evolve away from privilege and exclusivity and toward integration. The localization of universities, either in urban ghettos or exurban fortresses, makes no sense in view of today's social priorities. The city is the university; the university is part of the city.

Public transportation systems should be efficient and comfortable. In most cities they are antiquated, congested and beastly. They have not been kept up or adapted to changing patterns of urban activity and have developed conditions of intolerable stress as a result of their

il vous faut l'huile Lesieur

34. *Public transportation systems should be efficient and comfortable. In most cities they are antiquated, congested and beastly. They have not been kept up or adapted to changing patterns of urban activity and have developed conditions of intolerable stress as a result of their inflexibility.* Suburban station at Garges-Sarcelles, north of Paris, where some 30,000 new dwellings have been built under government subsidy in the past fifteen years. Passengers waiting for a train, before dawn, to take them to the city and their jobs.

inflexibility. '*Metro, boulot, dodo*,'* says the May 1968 grafitti in the Paris subway (in a paraphrase of the famous slogan of the Revolution: '*Liberté, Egalité, Fraternité*') – a cry of despair. But distribution of activities and use of contemporary technology in circulation systems could put the urban slave on the road to liberation. The reasonable distribution of activities within the reach of existing systems of transportation would already do much to alleviate the oppression of today's urban slaves. Why need they all work in one place and live in another distant place? Zoning of activities by areas has much to do with this, and it is easy to see how rezoning, or dezoning, could make cities more liveable. However, even with the

* Approximately: commute, work, sleep.

removal of all zoning controls (which we advocate) the city must be traversed continually by a vast number of citizens. We see no reasons why their necessary trips should be bad trips. We can assume that public transportation – mass transit – is the only sensible way to make the urban complex universally accessible. We would maintain that urban mass transit is one of the services which citizens naturally assume to be available to them, without unnecessary harassment. We should be aware that, among the unnecessary harassments, the individually paid fare looms large. Mass transit and the fare system are mutually incompatible. It is not reasonable to base a mass transit system on the premise of making it, and keeping it, inaccessible to the citizens by erecting coin-operated barriers. The mass transit systems should be 'free,' (i.e. supported by the city) just as other utilities such as roads and sewers are, or should be. To operate effectively they must be open to all, at all hours.

But beyond that, they should be attractive to the citizens. The Métro, the Tubes and the Subways (the burial of mass transit) represent a low point in our conception of how a city might function. 'Transport,' as Brian Richards says,* 'should have Delight.' There is no reasonable justification for having buried mass transit in the past, and none certainly today. Yet the newest American system, the Bay Area Rapid Transit system, perpetuates the error in making the crossing of San Francisco Bay in a tunnel when that, the best part of the ride, could have been made across the Oakland Bay Bridge. The decision was presumably based on factors other than human, although a mass transit system, finally, should subordinate all other considerations to the comfort (and Delight) of its passengers. Every mass transportation device should do its job in the most attractive way possible. That is its *raison d'être*: to attract passengers. If transit systems are systematically unattractive and become oppressive, then they are working against the forces which create them. We would, perhaps, be better without them. Certainly, poor mass transit is an anti-urban pressure, which tends to destroy the city, or to transform it into an unnecessarily unpleasant place. Many of us do not aspire to the role of urban slave.

* In *New Movement in Cities*, Studio Vista, London, 1966.

35. *Life in the city has been characterized by a kind of relentless promiscuity, a continual invasion of privacy, so that it is often lived largely on a defensive level. Some of this is surely due to overcrowding and congestion.* Paris, la rue Mouffetard on a weekday.

Life in the city has been characterized by a kind of relentless promiscuity, a continual invasion of privacy so that it is often lived largely on a defensive level. Some of this is surely due to overcrowding and congestion. 'Some thirty inches from my nose,' says W. H. Auden, 'the frontier of my person goes.' There is a field of study, called proxemics, with which Auden is certainly familiar. It has discovered, in animals, that when congestion becomes intolerable, suicidal tendencies develop. For the scientist who can hold himself aloof from the debilitating effects of everyday overcrowding, it is probably a comforting idea to think that, among animals, only man and the lemming will play out the overcrowding game to its irreversible end. Other species tend to correct their birth and death rates sooner, mostly by spacing out viable births. Although we cannot, apparently, do this by instinct (our instincts are perhaps too layered-over with knowledge), we may yet achieve population balance by reason – on condition that we understand our global common interest.

In the meantime, population increases are most immediately felt in cities, where the natural acceleration is compounded by immigration of displaced rural population. The urbanization trend continues, as far as we can see, and problems of congestion are certainly among the greatest which face us today. Of what use is it to reconsider zoning and to replan transportation if number is to be our nemesis? However, we can see from existing examples – Hong Kong, Tokyo, Paris – that density in itself is flexible. What is intolerable in Copenhagen might be typical in Tokyo. London might be more liveable if it were more, rather than less, dense. It depends on how services function and how the built world is designed. We can only be sure that we must in the future, in the best hypothesis, live with increasing numbers for yet a while. (The worst hypothesis would be a sharp reduction of numbers, through war or pestilence.) We must therefore plan to accommodate increasing numbers of citizens, without congestion. We can do this. We need not continue only to plan for life lived largely on the defensive level. We have sufficient intellectual resources to accomplish transformations of our social attitudes and actions so that life may be something more than existence and something less than constant aggression. Unlike the lemming, we have concepts of organization, and the potential to implement and change them.

Urbanism is much concerned with the alleviation of congestion, of course, but also with the need to make the public and private (and the semi-public and semi-private) domains coherent, to reduce the areas of possible confusion and conflict while yet allowing for the positive effects of integrated use of the entire urban fabric. The implantation of isolated housing projects in cities, or of dormitory towns, makes as little sense as the building of educational or industrial parks, or restrictive zoning for large lots. Public and private are contiguous and continuous, each supporting the other, but each clearly limited to its own domain. When the balance is not struck, when either clearly dominates over large areas, the fabric of life is discontinuous, creating zones of blight and reducing the possible benefits of urban existence to an ugly charade. The 'collective and individual binomial' of Le Corbusier, broken into separate components, and disconnected, makes no sense whatever, except as a flight from society back to a savage state. One of the most attractive aspects of Le Corbusier's urbanism, and architecture, is his affirmation of the need, first to insure privacy and then to wring out of the necessarily collective nature of the urban domain all of the benefits which it might secrete. There is a constant preoccupation with the individual-collective equation, a continual shifting of view from the particular to the general, from the general to the particular. In his way of thinking about urbanism, and architecture, one goes from one end to the other of the scale, in a kind of individual + collective social cost-benefit analysis. When either component dominates, the result is either a repressive or a chaotic environment, either mindless regimentation (in the subordination of the individual to the collectivity) or reckless proliferation of private interests to the ultimate disintegration of the social fabric. There is no longer enough territory for tribal (i.e. small-scaled) autonomy over marked-out hunting grounds. The benefits of collectivity today are not accessible to the tribe of fifty to a hundred; they are on the scale of the city of hundreds of thousands. But the change in scale brings with it an increased need for complete private control over territories which are clearly individual. In order for the collective to function well, the individual must be assured of his private, particular needs. A correct ordering, i.e. putting into a comprehensible order, of the activities which cities generate can promote the harmony between public and private uses which is essential to urban life, if it is to be worthwhile. In the situation of proximity, places must be assigned, and places left unassigned, if we are to organize our present and future activities and tranquillities in a beneficial way. To have tranquillity, one must provide for activity. The organization which takes both into account, as reciprocal parts, is the real structure of the city.

If the goals of urbanism are fairly clear, the means by which we may approach those goals are infinitely less so. The theoretical

36. *Urbanism is much concerned with . . . the need to make the public and private (and semi-public and semi-private) domains coherent, to reduce the areas of possible confusion and conflict while yet allowing for the positive effects of integrated use of the entire urban fabric.* New housing development on the edge of Paris. What is public, what is private?

37. *The implantations of isolated housing projects or of dormitory towns makes as little sense as the building of educational or industrial parks. Public and private are contiguous and continuous, each supporting the other but each clearly limited to its own domain . . . when either clearly dominates over large areas, the fabric of life is discontinuous, creating zones of blight.* Sarcelles: single-use zoning in the Paris region.

position is 'to change this, one must change that,' the implication being that nothing short of a complete revision of social, economic and political structures and systems will produce any effect ultimately. While a case can easily be made for such a total change (sometimes called revolution) it appears unlikely that present conditions in the west have yet reached the critical mass which would generate a revolution, if they ever do reach it, at least in the way we understand such things from history. There is no base sufficiently broad on which to build a revolution, in the sense in which that word has typically been used. Frantz Fanon, for instance, tried to show that all revolutions have been based on the rural mass, the peasants, although led by renegade members of the urban intellectual bourgeoisie. Since western countries no longer have this broad base of peasantry, he saw no hope of revolution in the self-styled developed countries. The urban proletariat, a relatively new economic class, lacks the cohesion which centuries of misfortune created in the peasantry. The urban prole may be no less oppressed, but because of his diverse regional origins (tribal differences), he is too susceptible to divisive tactics to be able to create a durable revolutionary mass. What we seem to be going through at present is a build-up of forces for rapid evolution, provoking a reaction from the forces for preservation of the status quo. The urbanist plays his role as a progressive but has to deal with essentially conservative administrators, in whose hands the power of decision lies. We say that 'to do that, you must do this,' but we are constantly reminded that 'this' is unthinkable, illegal, not feasible under the present rules of the game. However that may be, we keep in mind the fact that each millimeter of progress is better than no progress at all, and that progress in itself, even though it be apparently minimal, generates pressure for greater progress. Since we cannot use the blunt instrument with any efficacity, we must resort to the thin end of the wedge. The limits of the urbanist's effective action are, and probably will remain, extremely restricted, at least until he is able to demonstrate the social benefits inherent in his activities. And that demonstration will only be possible when a concern for quality in the physical environment is accompanied by a concern for the individuals who make up the social fabric. In other

38. *Each millimeter of progress is better than no progress at all, and progress in itself, even though it be apparently minimal, generates pressure for greater progress.* Projected development at the north-west corner of Central Park. The second level of pedestrian decks and bridges, an urban prototype, adds less than 1% to building costs. (Architects: Shadrach Woods and Bond, Ryder Associates.)

words, we will need to eliminate the disparities and inequities, to turn our backs on the beckoning delights of privilege, to counter and destroy vested interests. Can this be done, within the economic and political systems of the western countries? We must believe that it can, and we can point to the Swedish example, for instance, as a step in this direction, however faltering. Fourier and his theory of association is not entirely a dead letter: we have seen the kolkhozes and the kibbutzim come into being. The Island of Pines, in Cuba, a limited experiment in society without money, may provide us with further indications of the possibilities of associations which are not based exclusively on monetary gain, but on an exploration of human potential for social harmony in our new technological and numerical context.

Many examples can be given of small-scale attempts, in the capitalist context, to cooperate to the fullest extent in both urban and rural communes or communities. None of these are particularly significant from an urbanistic point of view. All of them are efforts, by people with little or no power, to function as a collective unit, at once within and outside of the current political and economic systems. Cooperation is seen as a way to increase or consolidate the small power which the cooperators may hold individually. Thus, buying- and selling-power over goods and services, and voting-power as blocs, are examples of cooperation. But these are always operating in direct symbiotic, although antagonistic, relationship to existing power structures and, in a way, draw their own small power from the continuing existence of those structures. In other words, most co-operative efforts have a vested interest in the perpetuation of the very abuses which they contest. They cannot then be seen as revolutionary, but rather as isolated and individual gap-stoppers.

We have long, perhaps too long, been accustomed, in the west, to delegate power into the hands of those who wish, for whatever reasons, to take on the increasingly awesome responsibilities of governing our societies. Decision-making has been institutionalized, and hence dehumanized, perhaps as an inevitable result of urbanization. The chairman, the president, the cabinet and the council, the members of parliaments, the colonels and the cops exercise increasing power (with decreasing direct responsibility), over our daily lives. Urbanism is part, a most important part, of our humdrum existence. Yet we have less to say than our ancestors did, about the decisions and indecisions, of ever-growing importance, which shape our local world. There is virtually no immediate user-participation in the debate over how the 'society' forms the built world. No public view is encouraged in the corridors of power, and matters of vital importance to the public, i.e. to everyone, are treated *sub rosa* between interest-peddlers. The public submits to, and suffers under, the yoke of urbanism-from-on-high. Our world is upside-down.

It seems clear that urbanism is, *par excellence*, an activity where the participation of the user, the ultimate client, is of the greatest importance. Yet it is carefully shrouded in mystery, and its simple intentions are obscured with jargon incomprehensible even to the professionals. One of the most deeply-felt protests of the May 1968 recognition in France and Italy was that which was raised against 'professionalism' and 'corporatism' in the planning and design professions. All at once, people realized that design decisions which affected their lives were being taken, not only without their consent, but even without any evident consideration of their needs, desires or aspirations. A great machine, a juggernaut, was rolling over them and the only hope for survival seemed to lie in cutting off its source of power and dismantling it. And yet its source of power should have been the power of the people. The professional skills in design which have been collected in ministries, administrations and authorities have surely no other use than to distill urbanistic decisions out of popular needs. Unfortunately, this use has not been understood fully, and the misuse of those skills to promote and to perpetuate a hostile, often repressive environment has led to the alienation of the people, and the consequent cut-off of this principal source of power and sustenance. Urbanists, architects, planners find themselves today on extremely shaky ground. Not for nothing was Estragon's ultimate insult: '*Architecte!*' And the Parisian *chansonnier* whose refrain was, '*Merde à Vauban!*' struck a chord of popular sympathy far beyond the potential of his pseudo-poetry. The architect-urbanist has become a symbol of repression.

We see that our effective action as urbanists is tightly circumscribed by the political and economic context. Working unimaginatively within that context, urbanists and architects have alienated their only potential supporters, the people. So doing, they have become the servants of institutions and corporations whose principal ethical position is: 'The people be damned!' And they – we – are building a world in which the people are, effectively, damned to a lifetime of compulsive acquisition of deadly 'consumer-goods' in at best, a nondescript environment, and at worst a frankly repressive one. We've all been 'playing the game,' with each other, excluding or ignoring the people whose lives the game affects. Urbanists and architects are only water boys in that game.

Perhaps all this will change. There will perhaps be born a consciousness of the problem of, and the need for quality in, urban life and in the physical milieu in which it evolves. However, we feel safe in predicting that it will not change in itself, or through the isolated morphological gymnastics of the urbanist-architect. 'To change this, we need to change that,' is still true.

We need, undoubtedly, to set our society free of the self-fulfilling prophecy that 'Quantity excludes quality' or that 'More is worse.' If any reasoning underlies such statements, it is surely spurious. Why should more be worse? Why should quantity exclude quality? Both these statements are founded on a snobbish myth which belongs to the synthetic aristocracy of the nineteenth century. One could translate them into 'anything that is good for people is no good,' a

39. *Why should more be worse? Why should quantity exclude quality?*
A child contemplating mass-products in Moscow department store.

statement that none of the holders of the above positions would be willing to endorse in public.

This entire argument is a false one, for if one reverses the terms and says 'Less is best' or 'Quality must be limited,' one finds oneself immediately adrift, cut off from the world, without any compass. The very notions of quality, and better or worse are irrelevant, in the sense in which they are used here. 'Less is more,' said Mies Van der Rohe, but as he said it he was defining and refining the use of standardized, industrialized elements in architecture. Jean Prouvé may do as much, and more, than Mies Van der Rohe, and he does it with considerably less. Both are architects of the first quality; that is to say, their buildings are positive and beautiful expressions of the highest, fundamentally human, aspirations of their societies. Both Mies and Prouvé (there are many others, but these are the leaders), have embraced modern technology in buildings without seeing it as necessarily dehumanizing. Their use of currently available materials to achieve results which are distinctly equivalent to the best examples of timber and masonry buildings, should serve as models to the urbanist. We need not abandon quality simply because we deal in quantity. We can use new mass technologies to make cities as graceful as any historical examples. But that is not to say that the use of those technologies guarantees that result, or that new is equal to good. The new techniques must be mastered, just as the old were, and put to good use.

Quantity does not exclude quality, and more might very well be better than less. Urbanists and architects would be well-advised to reconsider these dogmas and to concern themselves less with the ghosts of nineteenth-century taste and more with the potential, for beauty and appropriateness, of twentieth-century vocabularies. And, of course, included in those vocabularies is always the word 'user' and the phrases 'user-participation' and 'ultimate client.' We are perhaps working our way around the artistic delusions of the recent past, common to architects and urbanists, and back to the roots of architecture and urbanism.

There has long been accepted, and encouraged by government and corporations, a notion that architecture and urbanism are somewhat superfluous arts of embellishment, of the same family as painting and sculpture. They are considered to be costly and non-essential, when compared to such utilitarian pursuits as building and urban infrastructure. This extreme position, which dissociates architecture from building and urbanism from urban organization, has even been advanced by architects and urbanists. The *Beaux-Arts* establishment in France, for instance, used to make a virtue of its superfluity and irrelevance to contemporary matters. Architecture was the feather on the hat of a modishly dressed culture, an element of conspicuous consumption. Urbanism had to do with axes and monumental spaces. Le Corbusier's *Ville Contemporaine pour 3 Millions d'habitants* was his response to an invitation to present an urban design project 'such as a fountain' at an official exhibition. It marked, in the west, the beginnings of the movement back to the real concern of architecture and urbanism: the quality of human habitat on the urban scale. We are, essentially, the servants of the people, which sounds like another empty political slogan. Nevertheless, it is the only source from which architects and urbanists can draw any sustenance. If that is not our belief, then we are wasting our time and imposing a frightful waste on our ultimate clients. We are not doing anything *for* somebody, we are doing it *to* and *for* ourselves.

Architects and urbanists, if they are to be useful (not to mention successful) must go to the user and draw support from him. Those 'decision-makers' to whom we have conceded so many decisions, will be responsive only to popular outcry, if then. We can do nought with the decision-makers, unless we are backed by the popular voice. And if we are not backed by it, supported by the people whose lives we shape through building, then perhaps we should do nought. In such a momentous undertaking as the physical organization or reorganization of large pieces of the city and the design of the built world, we need all the help we can get. If we do not go to the user, as well as to technical experts, we run the risk of continuing irrelevance. But such is not our vocation. We are not, fundamentally, irresponsible form-givers.

We are experts in the distillation of form from a mash of conflicting needs and means, of goals and aspirations, of constraints and

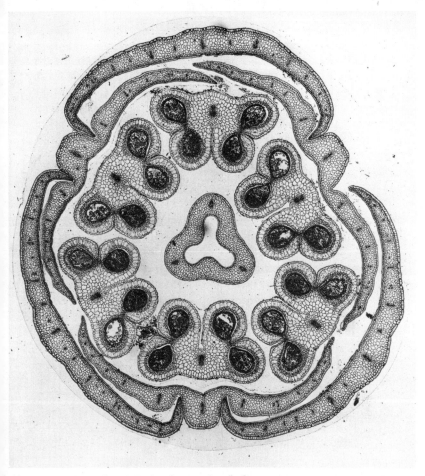

40. *Form ... is primarily organization.* Cross-section of a flower.

contradictions. Form, in this context, is primarily organization. As Le Corbusier said to the students of architecture, 'You are not drawing-board artists, you are organizers.' We exist to organize the physical environment in ways that work – if possible sweetly, if not, at least well. We work within economic (sometimes financial) and social (sometimes political) constraints. We also work within the laws of gravity and entropy, which are overriding, at least for the present. We are concerned with movement and with stillness, with communication and isolation, with natural and artificial environments, with ponderables and imponderables. We can define the goals of urbanism but we cannot yet discover the means by which we might approach those goals. We can − any fool could − enumerate the problems, but we are without ways to demonstrate the solutions to those problems. In this sense, urbanism is politics, i.e. the discovery and implementation of the means to a demonstrably desirable end.

We are often as unsure as any citizen of the demonstrable desirability of that end, which all means are meant to justify. However, we might even take on that enormous responsibility, were it not denied to us. As a result of our own lack of responsibility toward our professions, in letting architecture and urbanism move into the realm of superfluous embellishment where they become reserved to certain classes, institutions and corporations, we have abdicated the *beau rôle* in favor of an inconsequential walk-on part. The *beau rôle* is split up among other technicians and professionals where it usually perishes of incoherence. If architects and urbanists, whose vocation it is, will not assume the responsibility for the built domain, how can others who do not have the requisite disposition and training be expected to take it on? Having removed ourselves from the daily battle for a more than barely adequate environment we should not be surprised at having responsibility removed from us. And by removing from us responsibility, the institutions which govern our world, effectively reduce us to a decorative function, a useless appendix, to be readily eliminated. But we know better, we cannot easily accept this part of exterior decorator, sweeping great problems under a fashionable rug. The hope we have, the only hope, is to keep those problems out in the open, in the public view. Rugs may be pleasant; indeed they are; but when they serve to hide structural defects they can become deadly traps for the unwitting victims of society's irresponsibility.

In architecture or urbanism the disguising of poorly conceived programs to make them appear as novelties, worthy of note, and therefore worthy, is an unpardonable exercise. A program of construction remains unfocused, undefined in its details until it becomes a building. Planning programs are even more indefinite than building programs. The program may conceal, and the realization reveal, unsuspected snares. One must take great care to expose as clearly and as early as possible the intimate details of planning and building programs to public view, since it is evident that the buildings and urban environments which will grow out of those programs are inevitably of public concern. Power to the people, as the slogan has it, but also in matters of urbanism, which are necessarily of importance to the public, power must come from the people.

The rug of fashion does not wear well, even when it is laid on a perfectly good (and safe) floor. It can never be used to cover over a rotten structure, to conceal potentially fatal faults in the construction of societies or cities. Style is a fleeting commodity, at best a pleasant overlay on a solid base. We should be more concerned with the base than with the overlay, although we will all surely recognize that, among other qualities more tenacious, the quality of style – elegance – is important. It is our contention that this quality of style cannot be isolated from the more essential qualities of function and appropriateness in architecture or urbanism. When the attempt is made to consider it alone as important, as fashionable critics have tried to do in the past fifty years, the philosophical and humanistic basis of modern architecture and urbanism is ignored, and stylistic variations and deviations become the servants of mass advertising for more conspicuous consumption. The modern movement toward open planning for an open society becomes subverted to a kind of exclusive and fashionable life-style for continued class-conscious oppression. This is not, however, what we are about. It would be better to relinquish all claims to style, elegance and art; they are of little matter for the present and will take care of themselves in the future, when there is a solid basis of architecture and urbanism on which to hang them.

We need desperately to get back to the essentials of our professions – to the essence of architecture and urbanism which is far more stimulating and relevant than any issue of stark or lavish appearance. The essence is *organization*. We have before us so many problems and possibilities of new organizations, new scales, new systems, new attitudes, new aspirations, that the question of fashion (what is 'in' at the moment) seems scarcely worth our while. However, it is clear that government and institutions do react to the power of the press, but the western press has very few critics who have the courage, or the vision, to rise above sensationalism. Vast sums are squandered on unreasonable projects whose only attraction lies in the favorable attention which they have received in a press avid for novelty, while sensibly visionary proposals go to waste, ignored, rejected because not telegenic (or 'newsworthy'). We should by now have learned that that which is newsworthy is rarely worthy.

Architecture and urbanism are not consumer goods. The images of the future which pass in the press are fleeting, and may serve to sell soap, but they do a real disservice to the world of man by creating confusion in the minds of the decision-makers and inhibiting them from taking the unsensational steps which need to be taken. The architect, as a fashionable rug-peddler, catering to the critics' unavowed need for novelty, degrades his profession and erodes his useful potentials to society, in a game of who's who. It is unlikely today that any critic, no matter how perspicacious, can relive the adventures of Sigfried Giedion in the late twenties and early thirties. After all, Giedion did not invent Le Corbusier and the CIAM.* He

* Congrès Internationaux de l'Architecture Moderne. An international group organized by Le Corbusier and others to defend and promote modern architecture in 1928.

41. *The essence is organization. We have before us so many problems and possibilities of new organizations, new scales, new systems, new attitudes, new aspirations.* Expressway interchange in Chicago: new systems and new scales, creating new problems.

42. *Architecture and urbanism are not consumer goods. The images of the future which pass in the press are fleeting, and may serve to sell soap, but they do a real disservice to the world of man by creating confusion in the minds of the decision-makers and inhibiting them from taking the unsensational steps which need to be taken.* Paley Park, a vest-pocket park on 53rd Street in Manhattan. An unsensational urban step, taken by captains of industry, substituting for the administrative decision makers. (Paley, of CBS doing what the Mayor of New York should have been doing.)

just happened to be there, and realized the importance of the moment. But many good architects may be misled by publicity-minded critics whose hope is to relive that adventure, to be the Giedion of some new Le Corbusier. Architects and urbanists of the stature of Le Corbusier, and critics of the intelligence of Giedion are, however, rare. The media would do better to rest a while, until the combination repeats, probably in some inaccessible place, while nationalist teeth gnash with spite. In the meantime a great deal of nonsense will have been written about this or that mode or style or slogan.

We are paid then, to organize the built world; we are not drawing-board artists. The only way in which we can begin to do our work is by exposing to the public view the qualities and defects in the systems which govern the allocation and use of our resources. Urbanism, for the present, has been largely coopted by those systems in order that it may be used to continue and sometimes mask their inequities. Zoning ordinances and master plans are largely extensions and expressions of colonial systems. Colonialism begins at home, one might say.

Zoning is a pseudo-functional device for controlling land-use in the city. It is theoretically intended to resolve conflicts between mutually exclusive uses, such as dwelling and heavy industry, but is generally used to manipulate land value and to perpetuate privilege, or graft. Among contemporary urbanists, previous zoning is generally recognized to be counter-productive, i.e. it inhibits schemes which are generated by those of us who would see the city whole, and not as a fortuitous conglomeration of mutually exclusive activities. Zoning is an invention of city planners, perhaps a necessary one in its time. If there were problems in the functioning of the cities, which the zoning tool resolved, it is clearly seen today as an overkill weapon. The mere fact of assigning certain uses to certain areas, in view of our ecological awareness, is contrary to present urbanistic tendencies. We realize that we cannot escape pollution by concentrating industry in restricted zones. The problem is not to concentrate the pollution but to eliminate it, or to control it. Generally, however, zoning is no longer functional in this sense. It is used to protect private properties against depreciation by promiscuity. In other words, it is an instrument of oppression: in some countries of racism, in others of class distinction. Although contemporary planners continue to use this device, it is not clear that they really approve it. It seems to continue on its own momentum, and makes less sense, functionally, today than it ever did. Zoning remains; it perseveres through graphic, polychromatic indications on plans that planners produce. It has no correspondence in human aspirations, beyond the protective, anti-urban reflex to grow rich from the land, which is an absurdity, both social and ecological.

The way for urbanists to begin to put their skills to work in socially productive ways is not for them to go to the existing established sources of power from above, but to create new sources of power from below; to go into the streets and work with the people they find there whose lives depend upon the correct arrangements of the physical and economic milieu. To promote change in the systems of privilege and to combat the pernicious manifestations of those systems, we need first to expose clearly the links between one and the other, so that the argument for change becomes evident. Then we need to demonstrate, in a comprehensible way, what can be the effects of change. It would be fraudulent for us to advocate change for its own sake, or because a change could only be for the better. Such tactics are lame from the start and will only reinforce the position of a conservative power structure. However, we know why we want to change the systems of exploitation and we can learn how to make our knowledge speak to the people, who hold (at least potentially) the greatest power available. We can learn a great deal more in this dialogue with the man in the street than ever we could in the thickets of academe, and from that exchange of knowledge we can become more effective in our role as urbanists, organizers of the urban environment. We have skills which can be demonstrated (although they are not presently being fully used) and the urban communities have knowledge which we cannot have. The need for change in urban life is felt by all. The ways to produce change are limited and obscured by political legerdemain. We need to consolidate our skills and knowledge, urbanists and communities, so that we may together discover the ends to which we aspire and the means to those ends, which are now only vaguely apprehended. We will need to fight the systems of privilege which govern countries and cities, to take it all apart before we can put it all together, and the enemy is redoubtable.

Among other wiles which are used to maintain oppression and exploitation by the present system of privilege which we may cite, patriotism and the defense of the nation are old standbys, apparently with unflagging appeal to our basest instincts. They are used to justify a war economy, the use of restrictive tariffs and the siphoning off of funds to subsidize crass mercantilism, as well as other 'prestigious' activities. All of these malignant pursuits, which can only benefit the privileged members of an arbitrarily created system of oppression in which the power of the people is usurped, are customarily swathed in veils of patriotism. They constitute major obstacles on the road to a humanistic urbanism, for they are designed and used to concentrate wealth and power in the hands of a few, leaving little or no means available for the needs of the many, who are properly the concern of urbanists. This misuse of national wealth will have to be exposed to the public view, not in these vague polemic terms, but as the documented alternative to urbanism under the present economic systems of the west. There is probably not enough wealth available in most western societies to create a decent environment at home while destroying, or projecting the destruction of the environments of others abroad, whether it be through war or through economic imperialism.

The myth of economic expansion through proliferation of consumer goods will need to be dissipated also, before the right priorities of urbanism can prevail. The notion of expanding markets with ever-increasing needs is a mystical hoax which has been foisted upon us, almost as a religion, to the detriment of our societies and lives. It can be shown, we are sure, that waste does not necessarily make wealth. It only concentrates wealth and pollutes the earth. But by giving to the few a vested interest in the destruction of everybody's environment, it again furthers the short-term position of the privileged and extends the systems of inequity.

The urbanist and the man in the street will need documented arguments to bring down this house of marked cards, especially since the delights of privilege are lavishly offered to anyone who is prepared to become alienated enough from his society to wish to raise himself from the status of victim to that of oppressor, like the dwarf Alberich in Wagner's *Rheingold*. There is quite obviously not enough to go around; a society of people cannot continue to function by stealing laundry from each other, no more than it can by taking in each other's wash. The increment which makes the consumption-oriented, expansionist economy possible is obtained either by neo-colonialist 'economic' policies toward the other hemisphere, or by mortgaging the future through waste of resources and pollution of the environment, and usually by both.

To fight such formidable foes (they are not 'paper tigers') the urbanist and the man in the street, who desire to make a better physical and social environment for everybody at home and abroad, will need not only to be deeply committed to the realization of that desire but also to be well equipped with arguments to cut the fog and to formulate new ends and means. We will need other skills which are related to other disciplines, such as medicine, economics, sociology, philosophy, ecology, the physical sciences, agriculture and law. Most of these or all of them are now available to us. There is a feeling abroad in the air that touches everyone today, a suspicion that all is not for the best and that the time has come to change both 'this' and 'that.' Urbanists may have now a chance to act as catalysts for revolt in the general dissatisfaction with the results of uninhibited rapacity. They can do this by forming a coalition with the people, and with other trained professionals, and then distilling power from below to confront and contest the misuse of power from above. This coalition can perhaps establish, or re-establish, the right of self-determination in society, not only for individuals, but for communities. In the generation of power from below, the principal motive will necessarily be the right of self-determination for urban communities who are already self-conscious. We hope that the importance of this local appeal will grow into a consciousness of the rights of the urban agglomerate as community rights are established. We may first seek to convey power into hands of communities which already exist, but that is only a transitory stage. The reality of power in an urban community has already been demonstrated and is constantly being rediscovered. That power is always almost uniquely political, not financial. It has to do with votes and, as most things which have to do with votes, is mostly vocal. The politicians who lust for power to distribute patronage are extremely sensitive to vocal and vote power. The communications media, especially the newspapers, are ever eager to seize upon issues which come from the masses of urban discontent and to broadcast them. Our role in this conveyance of power is an advisory one in which we detect and reveal the issues which are not only worthy of discussion but also productive of dissent and confrontation. The confrontation technique which we have discovered in America and France, when associated with pressure upon sensitive parts of the political body will produce results that often go beyond the immediate issue. No politician wants to be identified as the enemy of the people (even though he be an apparently immovable power-broker). The only ultimate power which he can generate is popular support at the ballot box. The power thus conveyed should then be consolidated and redirected toward achieving not only local but city-wide and national goals. Otherwise we will probably see fragmented and frenzied intra-mural struggles of one community against the other, to the detriment of all. However we are convinced that the effort to achieve a redirection of national priorities can only find support if it begins by mobilizing local communities on the basis of their right to self-determination. They constitute the only potential pressure groups which can be mobilized immediately, and they probably can only be mobilized on the grounds of immediate and local benefit.

This is not to say that the right of self-determination in society is equivalent to the much more vague notion of individual liberty. The myth of individual liberty has too long been used as a cover for oppression, and to abolish social liberty, practically. It was ever a tactic, never a possible reality in an urban society. It was the rallying cry of affluent colonials, rebelling against centralized control; a far cry from the need of self-determination and community control which we feel today. Let us not be deluded by that bogus appeal; we have other concerns and virtually none of them can be contained in the American colonists' ideas of individual liberties. We do not, collectively, feel that our rights as individuals — be those individuals families, tribes, communes or other groups — can override the rights of a larger society which includes all of the groups possible or imaginable. It would indeed be reactionary for urbanists to represent the rights of independent individuals, and even more so to maintain those rights in the face of overwhelming social needs. It would be an aberration, although one which we have often seen projected as an ultimate social good in the land of the free and the home of the brave.

Individual liberty is to be prized highly, of course, but only to the extent that the liberty of individuals does not consist of inhibiting social harmony. As individuals, in today's world we are everything, we are nothing. Our individual liberty, the right to do as we want, can only be exercised at the most intimate levels. We may do as we like, but only so long as doing so does not prevent others also from doing as they like.

A current fashion for doing one's own thing may seem momentarily admirable, but one must remember that the bankers and corporations never did anything other than their own thing, which was to exploit and despoil. It is evident that there is, and must always be, in society a place for individual liberty. But it can never be a criterion of social organization, unless we wish to sink again into the morass of dog-eat-dog capitalist competition, from which swamp we cannot even see, much less pursue the *Fata Morgana* of legendary human association. Some of the dogs aren't eating; others are stuffed. Their concern with each other is only as potential nourishment, a view which we feel no obligation to encourage. It has made, and would make, for an exceedingly poor environment, both social and physical.

The feeling which is prevalent in western societies that something basic has gone wrong, is one which the urbanist and the man in the street can only welcome. We've known it for a long time; the urbanist because he finds himself acting contrary to his vocation, the man in

43. *The feeling is prevalent in western societies that something basic has gone wrong . . . the street is no longer his, no longer functioning as the life-line which he rightly expects it to be.* Street scene in Rome.

the street because his street is no longer his, no longer functioning as the life line which he rightly expects it to be. No amount of 'upward mobility' will restore to that street its life-giving function. Upgrading of a bare minority will not change the basic, and basically degrading, inequities of the systems which we allow to govern us. As the Swedish or German roadmender becomes a bureaucrat, ensconced on his leather cushion, and the Swedish and German governments see themselves obliged to import (slave) labor from around the Mediterranean basin to fulfill his needful function, it is not clear that anyone may be said to profit, in his humanity, from this exchange. A Swede becomes sedentary, a Turk is uprooted. No reason which obeys the rule of reason can be found for this game of musical chairs. In addition, sadly, there is no music.

We know that the bureaucracy, which deals only with ponderable factors, can outline for us the inevitability of such permutations, usually based on the American example. The maintenance of the public domain, e.g. the streets, entails labor costs which can be cut or eliminated. No attention is given to the essential social aspect of the job of roadman, to the necessity of maintaining the public domain, in which we are all concerned, correctly. In a reflexive reaction, based on the emulation of bourgeois attitudes, an important social function was casually destroyed, and those who performed it, degraded. Hollywood, and especially Chaplin, bore the message to the people that maintenance of the public domain was somehow unfitting work for fully-fledged members of the great democratic society. The process continues, and after the roadmen, the next most despised are progressively all the others who serve the society, until finally we lose view of the society itself, and value more highly the prime minister, or the president, who has himself become a highly suspect character, than the other keepers of the public domain. They are then only our domestics and he the wily, and corrupt, butler who rules their roost. Naturally in the process the public domain, physical and political, grows ever more neglected. And the impulse to turn to other social and administrative systems grows ever stronger. That impulse might urge us forward, to new and more open human associations, but it might equally push us back into severely structured, authoritarian regimes. For want of a society which can once again comprehend that the function of public service is a beneficial and rewarding one, we may easily lose the kingdom, and the city of man.

Commonly in the western world, what happens in America is right and just and, more importantly, inevitable. It is then taken as a model for what must happen in the rest of the west which, one must admit, has recently been massively and injustifiably dominated by the American example. But why should western European countries play the American game, according to American rules? True that America is the latest and most flagrant example of a northern European suicidal culture. Nevertheless, one would rather hope that the Europeans, seeing the extent to which unbridled folly could go, in the American example, would adjust their social mechanisms to avoid the pitfalls clearly before them. But no, they rush toward doom, always a few years or decades behind the great American model. The pied-piper of consumption for its own sake is apparently irresistible. We will make a better world for the already affluent few by destroying the world. As the young radicals, even in America, say, 'Is this a system?' and their disbelief in the virtues of such a system may very well, one day soon, outweigh their desire to live comfortably with what has gone before.

No, this is not a system, except that it is systematic repression aimed at maintaining an impossible *status quo*. Here again the urbanist will be hard-pressed to demonstrate how and why the system of privilege must and can be dismantled. A theoretical argument, which is easy to make, would say that since the system is unresponsive it must be dead, or very nearly so. However, like the scorpion, the system hoards its most deadly venom for its final agony. It may very well kill us before we are done with it. The system, which is not a system, but a spontaneous coalition of the forces of oppression, is the natural enemy of urbanism.

We have attempted to define urbanism and have tried to identify its essential goals. In a polemic way we have pointed out the general outlines of the means to these goals, and the obstacles which must be overcome in order to approach them. These essential goals of urbanism, the means to approach them and the problems which those approaches face may be considered at several scales of intervention. This device may, or not, prove more serviceable than the general polemic. The proof of our pudding will lie in its merits, of course, and given the same ingredients, other urbanists might make a more or less palatable mess of things. We've chosen to consider the goals, means, and problems of urbanism at four scales of possible intervention. We hope to suggest the possibilities of intervention at each of those four scales, which are: local (*in situ*, renovation); urban, (extension); regional, (problems of interconnection); and global constraints having to do with the integration of urban and rural problems. The program is vast. We can only hope to touch upon parts of it, which may be satisfactory since our real intention is only to raise questions about what is being done and to suggest ways in which it might be done better. We can't pretend to outline, from our limited knowledge, a program of world improvement.

No one is against urbanism; no one is opposed, overtly, to the idea that the ways in which cities and fragments of cities are designed should follow some basic principles and obey some basic laws which are flexible enough to change according to human needs or welfare. Among these principles and laws we can cite the need to reduce confusion, the need to determine what is public and what is private, the limits of private influence over public domains and vice versa, the need for tools for adequate servicing and for the criteria which control them, and the laws of mutability and adaptability.

Unfortunately, these principles or laws are rarely applied. One sees, and the case is not rare, the director of urbanism (city planning) displaying more concern for the baroque implications of a plan than for its organizational precepts. A commonplace, heard in all the governmental agencies which deal with physical planning, is 'Where is the center?' as though there should be an identifiable center in a contemporary plan. The anxiety underlying such a question is incomprehensible in a world which says it is dedicated to the ideal of an open society. One is obliged to conclude that the people in power are not at all dedicated to that ideal, or are woefully incompetent, or more charitably, one would say that they are confused. But confusion in places of power, where decisions affecting the environment of the entire society are taken, is inadmissible. It seems to be part of our bureaucratic destiny always, or almost always, to place the wrong men in these positions. Exceptions are rare and short-lived. One of the actions which some committed urbanists and architects might profitably undertake is to seek such positions, where they can, for a time at least, advocate the issues of common concern rather than those of private or special interests, as too often is now the case.

We are living in times which may properly be called revolutionary. Gradual change, correction of the course, no longer is possible for most cities of the west. Enormous pressures have built up as a result of too much temporizing with potentially radical situations. Our central governments, in Paris, London, Washington, the Hague, Rome, Bonn, etc., have all opted for an increasingly colonialist policy even within their home cities. Colonialism at home takes the form of capturing the wealth produced by the entire society and distributing it inequitably among the members of the society. The business of distributing the wealth produced by a society is operated through collection of taxes. When the 'take' in cash from any group exceeds the return to that group in goods, money or services, that group can be said to be colonized. The services include national functions such as health services, education services, environmental maintenance, international relations, and, some would say, national defense. This last has proved to be a particularly useful way of misdirecting the national product in ingenious ways, which all western countries have adopted with enthusiasm. Any country with a large military budget can consider itself internally colonized. Most are told, in outrageous addition of insult to injury, that they are not being adequately defended, and that more money is needed.

In all our capitals, decisions are made on the basis of expediency in an attempt to shore up the tottering structures of capitalist, free-enterprise exploitation. But those structures are deeply troubled. It is increasingly doubtful that they can be saved; there is, on the basis of their record, no good reason why we should attempt to salvage them from the fate of the dinosaur.

2. Inner City Renovation

The urbanist takes on many tasks, from the planning of new settlements to the remodeling of old ones. Among these, we may be sure, the most difficult is always the renovation of the existing central city. While the extensions of cities and the inter-connections between cities, new and old, may be seen as forays into unexploited, virgin territory; the preservation, renovation or replacement of rotted-out parts of the city itself, is increasingly understood as a necessary and complex task under today's social and economic conditions. It seems far easier (and it probably is) to deal with new settlements in virgin territory, where the urban blight has not yet taken hold, than it is to come to grips with the knotty questions of conservation, renovation and redevelopment of urban structures. And yet the latter is far more urgent than the former. The primary task, for urbanists, remains in the cities where most of the people live, in a complex, constrained and concentrated container, where most of the investment (material as well as spiritual) lies, and where new investment will necessarily produce the greatest return in both economic and social terms. In purely economic (and ecological) reasoning, if one is to conserve valuable resources, it is sensible to direct our major efforts to the city, where the greatest problems lie. Even though it may be possible, simultaneously, to envisage the development of new settlements and the renovation of old ones, we are sure that the priority must be given to the renovation of existing cities. And priorities must be assigned, as we are all aware. Priorities in national investment are the political way of life in the west.

Amid the shifting priorities which respond politically to local or vested interests, we would put the case of cities, as being of the most urgently preferential. The cities exist; the urban population is here;

one does not know whether or not the suburban phenomenon is permanent. Our first concern is with what we know, i.e. with the city, not with the guesswork of suburbia. And what we know about the city is, first of all, that cities are growing and changing. Cities change as they grow, and when they cease to change, they cease to live.

And so we would say that a great part of the urbanist's effort should be spent in the conservation of essential urban values, and to this end he should judge carefully what should stay and what should go. There are always many priceless cultural, historical and even monumental resources in the city which should be maintained at all costs. The dilemma, as always, is one of choice. Should the buildings

44. *The replacement of rotted, worn-out parts of the city itself, although increasingly understood as an activity, is much more elusive. It is far easier to deal with new settlements than it is to come to grips with the question of redevelopment and renovation on urban land.* Center of Frankfurt, which was burned out during the Second World War air raids, creating a rare opportunity.

by Baltard (the central markets in Paris) be maintained and rehabili-tated? And if not, what makes the Louvre (a mediocre collection of buildings) so sacred? Do we lose or gain more, in conserving the Louvre and demolishing the *Halles* than in doing the opposite (or in demolishing both)? It is clear, to any urbanist, that history and historical markers are important to the continuity of the city. No group, people or nation can hope to live without some continuity, and historical markers (or monuments) in the form of building are an important part of that sentiment. We would hope to conserve both the Louvre and the *Halles*, because both may speak to the citizens of past performance. It is less than rational to choose between them. It is criminal to sacrifice the *Halles* to growth and change (efficiency) and to perpetuate the Louvre as a symbol of glory and prestige. (The buildings which made up the *Halles* were far more prestigious, architecturally and technologically, than the rag-tag Renaissance of the Louvre.) But the eyes of administrators are unseeing, and the *Halles* are gone while the Louvre remains as a monument which no contemporary Parisian can appropriate. The point is not that one need choose between the two, but that urban renovation should neither be a mindless blotting-out of historical highlights, nor an equally mindless conservation of all that exists. The fact that Paris (i.e. the central government) made an unfortunate decision should only confirm us in our desire to renew the city without rejecting every-thing that is less than three hundred years old. Cities need renova-tion, to be sure, but they also need conservation. It is up to us to decide what measure of renewal or of conservation we will choose. The example of Paris (the destruction of the *Halles* and the conser-vation of the Louvre) may be an unfortunate one since one can logically argue for one or the other position, somehow. However it is clear to us urbanists that the casual destruction of the central mar-kets, in favor of a cynical land-use program based on the scarcity of land, was a real setback for the people and professionals who might argue for a more sensible use of the city's center.

In the *Halles* debacle we have witnessed a triumph: once again the force of ignorance has triumphed (under a banner of financial gain) over the forces of urban economy and, more importantly, of urban ecology. Artificially generated 'land value' has become more important than public interest. Paris is a city of some 6,000,000 persons. Yet under the obsolete rules of capitalism, it has been determined (by the central government, largely composed of private bankers) that these thirty or forty acres of the central city – which belong, *ipso facto*, to the 6,000,000 – are too precious to be developed as part of

45. Aerial view of an Italian town: Luccia in Tuscany, Italy.

the city, for the public good. In the land-value game they become inaccessible to the public. One yearns for a return to the empire of Napoleon III when these acres were clearly understood to be public property to be developed in the public interest. Our peculiar economic theory precludes any sort of rehabilitation or conservation of this essential part of Paris. The only economically sound proposal (under the current rules of the game) would seem to be to turn this place into another office building, higher and deader than its predecessors. No thought is given to what the center of Paris, the nexus of a web of communications, could mean to the Parisians. The only consideration, under a regime of bankers, is financial return.

And so we might return to the Louvre, and to propose that that disparate collection of buildings in bad taste, often execrable, be removed to make way for this wonderful new world of economic progress. The Louvre, in New York terms, is no better than what New Yorkers call a 'tax-payer,' i.e. a two or three-story building whose revenues are sufficient to pay the property taxes while the proprietor watches his property appreciate. Except that the Louvre, as national property, does not even pay taxes.

One wonders why the Louvre should remain, inviolate, while the *Halles* are callously destroyed to make way for more profitable investment. Does not this inconsistency demonstrate a flaw of capitalism? Or should we be content with such decisions, admitting that someone knows best, and hoping that he does?

I am inclined to say that that someone does not really know what is best, that he could not, and that the decision to destroy the *Halles* and to conserve the Louvre comes not from any clear-sighted appreciation of their intrinsic value but from an eternal compromise between what is good and what is seen to be universally accepted, as good. The Louvre, those endless, uncomfortable rooms, is accepted, so much to the good. Our quarrel would be with the conservateurs who cannot, or will not, convey the same distinction on the *Halles*. For after all those market buildings were, and are, architecturally more significant than that museum.

In the past, change and renovation of parts in cities proceeded at a pace somewhat less rapid than that of change in the social and economic activities and orientations of the citizenry. The changes that took place were experienced over decades and at first only concerned the gradual adjustment of the physical milieu to slight increases in numbers, or to minor variations in social and economic conditions and in administration and financing procedures. Now, suddenly, change is no longer imperceptible and no longer concerned only with small increments. Urban civilization has been revolutionized not only by industrialization, but also by basic changes in attitude. The city is changing in all its structures as well as in its composition. What formerly took decades to accomplish now takes years; more importantly, the decisions which formerly were in the hands of a continuing, identifiable aristocracy are now left to a shifting mass of bureaucrats, faceless and fundamentally uncommitted. The bureaucracy of government, institutions and corporations, is perforce uncommitted. The attempt, in the best of interpretations, to keep government honest has led to such a diffusion of responsibility that the working members of the administration find themselves constantly frustrated in their desire to perform adequately. When they seek to override the built-in checks in order to achieve or attain objectives which are clearly in the public interest, they run grave risks of attack, not only from opportunist politicians but also from fellow bureaucrats. We have thus invented a system which crushes initiative, rejects imagination and reduces human potential to desolate conformism. Clearly, in the process, we've outwitted ourselves. The mentality of the *apparatchik* derives not from his lack of dedication or talent, but from our having boxed him in through constant mistrust and scorn of his best efforts. We can see how this policy works to our disadvantage every time we try to grasp the problems of the city, but we persist in it. And yet, in all cities in the west scandals and frauds abound, put on public view at election time, ignored most of the time. We should allow our bureaucrats more responsibility, not less, so that they could rise to their vocation as public servants. The scandals will still be available for electoral purposes but the quality of administrative work can only improve.

It is evident that any human enterprise needs infusions of new blood and new inputs of energy to keep it alive. It is equally clear that

46. *A city is such an enterprise, and certainly may be thought of as a building. Change and decay, and replacement to accommodate change and to repair decay, are fundamental to the continued existence of the city.* Split, in Yugoslavia, showing the city built in Diocletian's palace.

any building, no matter how well conceived and built, needs maintenance and replacement of parts to keep it in a state of useful repair. A city is such an enterprise, and certainly may be thought of as a building. Change and decay, and replacement to accommodate those changes and to repair that decay, are fundamental to the continued existence of the city; a form of human association which may present many disadvantages of this sort, but one which seems at least to be endemic and necessary to civilization. To suggest that we can let the cities rot, or turn them into concentration camps for the poor, is to propose a view of society which is not only extraordinarily short-sighted but also repugnant to what are supposed to be the western civilization and ideals. Urban civilization should not necessarily be considered as a fertile field for the development of ideologies, which generally seek to cover too much ground to be really useful. Nonetheless we have been saturated with the idea that the motor of western civilization is the ideal of making a better world for everyone. The current tendency to segregate the suburban rich from the urban poor works in direct contradiction to that ideal. It is, then, against our alleged principles. It is also short-sighted in that it generates useless social conflicts, as the segregation of rich and poor must always do. Pulling the support of society as a whole out from under the city does not solve any suburban problems, but it does create new urban ones by reducing the financial potential of the city and making it more difficult for the city dweller to achieve a level of parity in services and environmental quality with the suburban neo-colonist. Both support and draw their sustenance from the city, yet the one is seemingly short-changed, continually and at every level, while the other suffers the illusion of affluence as a compulsive consumer.

There was a time when the contented purring of the motors of capitalism could cover the groans and shrieks of a down-trodden population, both urban and rural. Today, although the purr has become a high-pitched whine, the noise of money being made can no longer hide the obvious inequities and strains which are imposed upon urban populations. We have allowed, even encouraged, the systems of government and subsidy to transplant all of our national problems to the city. People have been transferred, in the name of efficiency and progress, from their poor livings in the country to even poorer lives in the city. Progress and efficiency should imply a net social benefit. One would be hard-put to demonstrate the social benefits of recent rural emigration in western countries, and one might say that the massive dislocation of agriculturally-oriented persons in the last century has not proven a conclusive case for progress and efficiency, in human terms. It has however, concentrated many problems in urban centers.

Cities grow and they change. Under the impetus of rural dislocation programs, which are ubiquitous in western countries, the
population of cities – those 'great cities' of external and internal
colonialism – tends to grow more rapidly than the population of their
countries, which is largely limited to the excess of births over deaths.
The result is a considerable strain upon the urban fabric, especially
when cities are considered as being distinct economic entities, self-
supporting and floating free of the total national or continental
economic system. Cities have become, in a sense, the rug under
which the national dust is swept. Internal colonialism is reversing
itself: instead of a country exploited by cities, we now see cities
colonized by their countries. The city has today become a funnel for
channeling funds (wealth) from the citizen who produces it to the
conglomerates which use it. The conglomerates include government,
institutions and corporations. The redistributors of wealth, such as
government and war industries, draw from the entire nation, but
spend locally. Thus we see New York tax money producing wealth
and prosperity in Houston, and the citizen who would participate in
any kind of equitable fashion must perforce follow the money. Unfortunately it is not given to New Yorkers to uproot themselves so
easily as to profit by, or even to survive in this system. So we have,
and one wonders why, poor New Yorkers and rich Texans.
Similarly we have seen vast farm subsidies supported out of national
taxes. Clearly the 'farmers,' among whom we count some US sen-
ators, have achieved an exploitation of the cities and their wealth,
which far surpasses any colonial impoverishment scheme yet seen.
Those 'farmers' to whom we make payments for not farming – a
particularly degrading form of welfare – are not even contributing to
the national wealth; on the contrary they are conscientiously sub-
tracting from it.

This reversal of the yoke of internal colonialism makes not only
for quantitative but also for qualitative change in the city. The
population composition changes; the social structures change;
political organization and economic function also change. Today's
citizen is truly a new man in a new world, although perhaps not a
world entirely of his choosing. He is more often than not personally

(i.e. psychologically) alienated by it, since he cannot find the ways to appropriate it to himself. He cannot be expected to understand that the role of passive victim of elusive, shifting *national priorities* is to be considered a worthy one for him to play. He cannot be expected to believe that urban deterioration is worthy of being endured in the interests of national product and prestige. But here he is, in the city, oppressed by it and full of justifiable resentment as he sees the government turn away from his problems to try and solve those of his less or more fortunate brothers in far countries. It cannot be demonstrated to him that present national economic priorities will necessarily make a better world for himself or for his children or, for that matter, for anybody's children.

He is a new man in a new world, and surely that world could be made better for his children, or even for himself. The making of a better world, which will of necessity be urban, is not an impossible task. Given the possibility, urbanists and architects will know how to do it, in so far as the built environment is concerned. Economists will recognize that a nation cannot exist as a functioning economic entity if it distorts so flagrantly its priorities as to maintain a system where some, or any, percentage of the population must suffer inhuman conditions in its daily life. Politicians will be aware of the dangers inherent in fostering a new colonialism. Sociologists are on hand to argue the needs of the people. Apparently all that is needed is the desire to work for socially productive change in that most changing place, which is the city.

The changes which must take place are those occasioned by the changing conditions around us, in the city. They will take place at a more or less rapid rate, depending on the strength of popular dissent with the *status quo*. We say that they will 'take place,' which conveys a sense of inevitability, but changes may also be made to happen, or may be impeded from happening, for reasons of public or private benefit.

The new man, in a new world, needs new conditions of life. He needs a change from the old conditions. But the need and desire for change is always accompanied by an opposite and nearly equal resistance to change. Western societies have long been addicted to

47. *The new man in the new world needs new conditions of life. He needs a change from the old conditions. But the need and desire for change is always accompanied by an opposite and nearly equal resistance to change.* Residents of Forest Hills, Queens, New York, demonstrating against the construction of new housing in their area.

the idea of constancy, often expressed as tradition. Conservatism is a force, a way of life for many. 'They change their stars, but not their hearts, who sail across the seas', said Virgil. It may be argued that the ruthless uprooting of agricultural persons should at least make provision for the conservation of their traditions. But how to conserve a rural tradition in an urban milieu? It is doubtful that it could be done, even if it could be shown that it should be done. However, this argument is superficial, and only used as a metaphor for the more profound and widespread feeling that any change must surely be for the worse, since almost all observable changes have been, in effect, changes for the worse. It is sufficient for our purposes to note that change has a reciprocal in the desire for constancy, and that every change may not necessarily be seen universally as a change for the better. The evolution of the new urban aggregate, now including many more origins than before, will be a product of a dynamic interaction of the forces for change and those opposing it. The citizen of the abiding city will also abhor change, even while desiring and submitting to it. For the desire for constancy, which takes the form of opposing specific changes, has the effect of producing other, unsuspected, changes. In the city, change is ineluctable.

Our concern is with the control and guiding of ineluctable change, in ways that might produce a change for the better. If change cannot be avoided, and it cannot, then how to make that change socially productive is our principal objective. How to use the force for change to further the ideas and ideals which we know or suspect to be productive, socially? And how can we know the ways to do that?

The answer is that we shall have to guess at the ways in which change might be channeled so as to produce effects generally believed to be socially beneficent. This guesswork has some supporting infrastructure, largely inherited, and some guidelines in historical examples, as well as in behavioral science theories and in humanist philosophies. There are many pitfalls on the course, which have been charted for us already and described in writings on urban life and form, and these will certainly provide valuable indications of what not to do. See, for instance, Jane Jacobs (in *Death and Life of American Cities*, Random House Inc., New York, 1961) and others. Many people have written of the deadly effects of unguided change in the urban scene. These writings tend, inevitably, to cite examples of what not to do in a picturesque situation, showing how ill-considered planning directives can destroy, along with a dying culture, the enduring, universal social qualities of a given environment. Generally the message which comes through is that to touch a stone of an established urban quarter would be to destroy it entirely, and with it a certain quality of urban life. Most of these writings, which have great popular appeal (like guidebooks on sex) propose only, in the end, to let popular misconceptions stand, to do nothing, and thus they are finally not only unproductive but downright malignant.

A more important question than what not to do, is '*How* not to do it?' When we know what to do, we may legitimately seek ways of realizing that knowledge, and of implementing clearly desirable programs. We can say, for instance, that public transportation systems should be improved, and we can even be quite precise about the ways in which some specific existing systems should be improved. We can then establish programs to carry out those improvements, and seek funds to support those programs. All of this is in the realm of practical policy making, which needs only to be recognized by the citizens as having priority at any moment in order to become effective.

Equally we can identify other parts of the urban infrastructure which should be maintained, improved, extended or completed. Roads, streets and footpaths, parks and playgrounds, supply lines and sewers, educational, social and health services, police and fire departments – generally all the systems of services and circulation

48. *We can identify parts of the urban infrastructure which should be maintained, improved, extended or completed.* Renovated park and playground in the south Bronx, New York. (Architect: Charles Jacob; Landscape Architect: George Cushine.)

within the existing urban fabric can be monitored. Necessary or desirable changes can be programmed. Here again an order of priorities should be relatively easy to establish, if the people are sufficiently informed as to the necessity and desirability, and the economic and social cost-benefit analyses of such programs, which may be improvements to or maintaining of existing systems of life-support.

In general, we may say that we know what to do to preserve these existing lifelines of urban agglomerations as long as we know the uses which they are to serve. But it is this very question of use in the urban fabric which is most difficult to establish. Clearly the building, which is the city, tends to wear out, or to change its use, or both, in parts which are more or less extensive. Those parts must then be replaced, or rehabilitated, and in order to renew parts of the building we need to assign uses to areas and volumes. The uses to which those rebuilt areas will be put determines, in turn, the characteristics of the systems which will service those rebuilt sections of the city.

We cannot provide manufacturing areas without providing adequate power and service, or office space without providing adequate access systems for peak loads, or residential use without schools, shops and parks, or any of these without connections to the others. However, in this partial redistribution and reorganization of the activities of the city, our guidelines are much less precise than in the design and maintenance of systems to serve them, and we tend to rely on such sparse information as that supplied by those who attempt to measure 'trends,' extrapolating from uncertainty.

The danger for the urbanist, of econometry related to geography, may often seem like a virtue. That imprecise non-science (in the guise of science) should remove his own insecurities and often does, and it replaces them with computerized, self-fulfilling prophecies, which are dressed-up, impressively, as projections. We should not, of course, dismiss out of hand the attempts which have been made to map future patterns of activity through the collection of facts about past patterns. However, we should be extremely wary of the numerical security which such prophecies offer. They can only be based on obsolete information, for instance, and they cannot accommodate imponderables. We have not yet learned how to evaluate seemingly remote and insignificant factors, such as wilfully obscured legislation on tax practises, nor how to relate these to urban development. Reasoning from cause to effect and observation of trends, while seeming a comfortable analytic perch from which to view a broad picture of possible futures may often be, in fact, a delusion. In one country the flight of industry from the city to suburban or exurban sites may be seen as a continuing and debilitating trend, with the center of gravity of the labor market remaining at the center of the city. While in another, the decentralization of industry is seen as a key to future happiness, although the trend shows no tendency for this to occur. Planning from the trend, in both cases, would undoubtedly prove to be disastrous, and so a policy must be adopted to fight the trend in the public interest as the planners see it.

The planners are, at this precise moment, more concerned with what not to do than with the acceptance of what their expert advisers tell them are the realities of a given situation. And that advice is abundantly documented with 'updated' projections. An updated projection is one that extrapolates from previously constructed tables, changing some figures in ways which are judged on their probability. It is an extremely problematic kind of guessing game, relatively unsophisticated, which takes its credibility from the fact that it is, after all, dealing with numbers. The numbers have been passed and repassed through information-processing devices, but all too often the input has only a very tenuous relationship with reality, and the output none at all. We have fallen victim to the myth of mathematical infallibility. When one examines the process, and sees with what imprecision the original data (on which the rest is built) are gathered and evaluated, one can see that only rarely are the impressive resulting figures to be given any credence. Their value lies not in their accuracy but in their power to persuade administrators into taking actions which will prove their accuracy, or worse, to justify previously determined actions. This method of decision-making is really a new mysticism, one which is felt to be more suitable to contemporary attitudes than the old way of intuitive, quasi-logical guesswork. But in fact, it is doubtful whether it describes any greater validity than the old, intuitive way. At least, it has yet to be conclusively demonstrated as more significant. It does, however, provide greater shelter from responsibility and a certain camouflage for urbanists who are determined to impose their theories on society.

There is no security in numbers of this kind even though there may be some temporary comfort in sheltering under IBM's vast grey umbrella. Despite the technocratic hocus-pocus which provides an impenetrable shield from public view of the proceedings, one suspects that the real decisions are still made in the old way, based more on the traffic of interests than on this new pseudo-scientific information.

For the urbanist, the question is how to renew a deteriorating urban area in the light of the uncertain nature of the information available to him. We may propose to accept the projections of Trend, and in so doing to try to make them come true. We may with equal validity, choose to construct what seems to be a desirable scenario of the future and try to make that come true. In both cases we are contributing to the making of policy, generally knowing little of what might be the effects of that policy on the lives of the citizens who must endure it. We may take another line and suggest that the problem is perhaps a false one, and that the need for such momentous decisions may not be as critical as it has been assumed to be. In taking this latter course, we involve ourselves in the discovery, not of how to do it, but of how not to do it. That is, how not to commit and compromise the future, how to avoid making an urban world which perhaps no one really wants, or will ever want. We know that changes will take place, or will be made to happen, continually. We have very little solid ground from which to launch a program of massive change. We might then be prudent, and avoid making unnecessary changes today which can only impede necessary changes in the future.

The idea underlying our reluctance to change that which needn't be changed is that it may be more important – it probably is more important – to conserve certain areas of the city, perhaps for future change, than to destroy and reconstruct them hastily. The need for change is obvious in many parts of the built world. The need for constancy in man's environment, both physical and psychic, is also important. And perhaps most important of all is the need to keep open the ways for future generations to effect the changes which they will see to be necessary.

The idea suggests that urbanists will need to discover how to make the change, which we know to be necessary, without removing options for future change. This is what is meant by 'How not to do it.' It involves the search for systems for change and growth which are open: non-definite, where the elements of definition are lacking; non-representational, where there is nothing to represent; non-centric, where there is no clearly identifiable central function. Such an attitude implies as much respect for the future as for the present, or the past. Just as we do not wish to be tied down by obsolete tradition, so we should not seek, even inadvertently, to constrain others, in the future. We may feel that we represent a new man in a new world, but we have no reasonable basis for assuming that our new world is the definitive and best expression, in qualitative terms, of a long evolution. It will certainly be an old world to the following generations. There is no golden age; there are only succeeding ages.

This is not to say that we should hide our own responsibilities in the future, by a tempting forward flight of fancy. We do not have any competence in dealing with the city of the future. If we have any competence at all, it is to perceive our cities' present problems and to deal with those problems expeditiously, today. That is all we can do, and it is an enormous task. As 'government' increases, bureaucracy increasingly seeks to avoid responsibility. Here, at least, is one instance where more is really less. When the bureaucracy is faced with the need to act on specific situations, its reaction is to push the problems into the future. We do not believe that urbanists should take the same tack. It is more important to rise to the present difficulties than to proclaim a future paradise. It is especially important not to allow present difficulties to continue and to ripen into future impossibilities.

At some time in the past, a collective decision was made, by a

49. *We may feel that we represent a new man in a new world, but we have no reasonable basis for assuming that our new world is the definitive and best expression ... of a long evolution.* Boston, urban renewal.

society which we might call primitive, that western civilization would be urban. The descriptive words – civilization, urban – testify to that. That point in time is not necessarily accurately definable, but our destiny has nonetheless been determined. We no longer have an option, a choice between an agricultural, rural, pastoral orientation and an industrial urban environment. We are, willy-nilly, committed to the built world, the man-made environment. It has become fruitless to speculate on such matters as 'what if we all returned to the earth, and nature?' Those doubtful pleasures are reserved to an extremely limited portion of the population, perhaps only to those who will accept willingly to become a counter-culture, which of course suggests acceptance of the culture to which they are counter. Our problems are urban; our culture is oriented to the city, a place where all can again participate, as perhaps once they did when living on the land. But again, speculation is idle and perhaps, since history, as René Sédillot* says, has no sense of direction, we might see a return to fragmented rural activity rather than a continuation of concerted urban activity. It would be difficult to conceive of such a reversal, and pernicious in the sense that we might then let our urban problems run on, for they will not eventually disappear. For our present purposes, we would prefer to admire and applaud those who take the route of return to the land, and be grateful to them for making clear to us some of the causes and effects of the psychological alienation of city dwellers.

The city in the past has typically been used for private profit and to serve special interests, whether these were political or commercial. We are at the point of realizing and proclaiming that the city is not simply a tool and manifestation of capitalism, but also an environment, an ecological entity. The new man's new world is a built environment, artificial in a sense: the city. With the change in elementary social structures, the city changes. It becomes the locus of the new man's activities and the expression of his life style and his aspirations. It is natural to him, no longer artificial. And it is normal that the city should change to reflect those social and ecological changes. The citizen begins to appropriate to himself the space of the city, and to realize that he and his activities and aspirations form the built environment. From now on so to speak, he is in charge; it is his world; the king is dead. From now, his decisions will determine the shape of the physical environment, and the scope of the communications systems, and the densities and intensities of activity within

* SÉDILLOT, RENÉ, *L'Histoire n'a pas de sens*, Librairie Arthème Fayard, Paris, 1965.

the urban fabric, at least for a time. The citizens are recovering and discovering their cities.

This is true for North America surely, and perhaps ancient history for north Europe. America and Europe share not only a common cultural heritage but also a common sense of approaching urban disaster, which is generated by the enormous changes which have been wrought in the distribution of people and activities over the past decades: the industrial revolution, the agricultural revolution, the health and population revolution and, of course, the concomitant revolution in social attitudes. The sense of imminent disaster comes more from our unfamiliarity with these new facts than from what we can know of the facts themselves. Given so many revolutions, we should rather be looking forward to a new era of urban development than to an endless deterioration of the inherited urban fabric. If we think of our cities as new worlds to 'colonize,' or as new phenomena to investigate, rather than as diseased and moribund relics, we may be able to detect the possibilities in them which thus far have been obscured by intimations of catastrophe. 'New cities are generally old cities' said Le Corbusier, but this is only true in the geological and geographical sense. Our cities may remain where they are, being there for many good reasons of geography, topography, climate, communications, etc., but they are really new in their social, political and economic organizations, as well as in their demography. The cities remain while their population changes. Population changes have been so radical over the past decades, with the uprooting of rural, sedentary persons that we may look forward to a renascence, rather than to a wake. There is an upsetting of traditional attitudes and values but this does not necessarily mean that the future is bleak for

50. *The city is not simply a tool and manifestation of capitalism, but also an environment, an ecological entity. The new man's new world is a built environment, artificial in a sense.* New development at Columbus Circle, New York City.

51. *The citizen begins to appropriate to himself the space of the city, and to realize that he and his activities and aspirations form the built environment. From now, he is in charge; it is his world; the king is dead.* The Dam in Amsterdam.

all. It is certainly unsure for those who traditionally viewed the city as their personal or corporate fiefdom, but they are few, and have removed themselves into the limbo of irrelevancy in any case. And, of course, along the way they chose not to live there anyway. They are now not only irrelevant but inexistent, and are touting Trend as the ultimate justification for their disappearance into the surrounding countryside. To see, and to provide, hope for the city we need only to consider that it is the new home of a new man, and he can no more conform to old urban stereotypes than he can take for his own the values of his predecessors or oppressors.

Cities are not only, or not even essentially defined by their physical milieu, still less by their plans. They reflect the preoccupations of their citizens and their character is determined not by their geometries but by the activities which those geometries serve. In a changing world, it is natural and normal that the cities, their populations and activities, lead the change. This should not be a cause of despair, but rather for hope, since the changes which we can describe are generally felt to be desirable, in the context of national development policies.

The new man and the new city which is his, will doubtless complement each other; the man forming the city, while it deforms him. In the past, other men, new men of their time, shaped cities. We assume that they formed them for their own good reasons, and we even go so far as to say that we can understand some of those reasons. One, which we often cite, was the reason of physical defense: safety in numbers. Another was the cooperation in other fields than defense: mutual profit in numbers. A third was social promotion (as we would call it today): to get closer to the shifting source of power. The source of power in those days was almost uniquely aristocratic and often by divine right. But it shifted from place to place, unquestionably obeying unwritten political laws, moving from the rural to the urban scene as improved communications made possible greater concentrations of power and fiefdoms were assembled into states and countries.

It could be that our reading of the history of cities is somewhat simplistic. Great human movements have their origins, their impetus, and their reasons in the complexity of human needs, desires and

52. *Cities remain where they are, but they are really new in their social, political and economic organizations . . . population changes have been so radical over the past decades, with the uprooting of rural, sedentary persons that we may look forward to a renascence rather than to a wake.* New York street with new man in new world.

53. *One reason (for the formation of cities) which we often cite, was the reason of physical defense: safety in numbers.* Rembrandt, *The Night Watch.*

aspirations. We can probably chart some of these needs, such as the ones mentioned above, but others are more elusive although perhaps nonetheless forceful and effective. We can think, for instance, of emulation: the liberated serf following the movement even after he has become free to choose, simply because his former masters and social betters were moving in a direction which they may have been able to apprehend, but which had little or nothing to do with him or with his livelihood. We can think also of psychological dissatisfaction with rural life, which surely must have appeared as soon as a glamorous alternative became available. We can think of other, more obscure, reasons that reason itself might well ignore.

It is significant to note, however, that many of the more obvious reasons, which we credit for the move to the city in the past, are virtually identical with the reasons which are given for a more recent move from the city toward a new low density pattern of suburban or ex-urban development today. There no longer seems to be, for instance, any safety in numbers. Indeed many of the more affluent city dwellers move to the suburbs to escape from anonymity and the terror of numbers. Against that terror, their only hope is either a bulwark of police and private armies, impossible to sustain, or headlong flight to an area where the reduced numbers of a low-density, scattered development seems to promise another kind of social security. Again, improved communications, and especially the motor-driven private vehicle, make possible the move to low-density residential districts. Of course, this kind of scattered development is only possible with automobiles and it necessitates a mobilization of wealth which can only be qualified as colonial, i.e. the use of natural resources of space and energy for private, individual benefit rather than for public, collective needs. Or again, the profit motive today militates against great urban concentrations of people as economic costs appear to rise at a greater rate than the population curve alone would indicate. The coming of social consciousness and responsibility like the invention of the police, also leaves the richer classes with a choice of either effectively participating in this social consciousness, submitting to it, or removing themselves from its reach.

There is then, really a new man in the new urban world. He is the man who is left behind, or who chooses to remain behind, after the exodus of the ci-devant bourgeoisie (for whom we shall have to find another name). But the new urban world is not a desert. It is full of old urban things, systems, structures and attitudes. To make it new, and fitting, we see the need to mobilize the wealth and energies of the entire society, in order to repair and renovate these systems and structures. Unquestionably the cities which are left to us, the new men, as the old privileged classes move on and out, are in a serious state of disrepair. Massive reinvestment is needed, as our urban administrators never tire of telling us. One should ask whether or not the decay can be stopped, and how, but also whether or not it is within our human possibilities to stop it.

Is not the new exodus an indication of the death of cities? Is not the collective aspiration now away from cities as we have known them, and toward new forms of scattered communities in more manageable numbers? I believe that we can show that this is a false issue. Urban population is not declining, although it is changing. The old urban middle class is on the move, scattering itself to, and beyond, the fringes of the city, while the less fortunate (less wealthy) gravitate toward the center. The economic system of exploitation of one part of the population by another does not change. There is money to be made in the suburbs, where new and cheap land can be 'improved' with cheap building and resold at great profit. The financial possibilities are enormous and the financiers have organized a vast campaign to create and manipulate a market where none existed before. The possibility derives from new means of communication, such as the private motor car and the telephone and radio, and television technology as well as tax benefits. The market is manipulated conscientiously through mass media campaigns depicting, on the one hand the good life of the ex-burghers, and on the other the dangers and incoherences of the city, which has become, in this scenario, no fit place for family life.

This is a present manifestation of the old desire of the more affluent (or rapacious) citizens to set themselves apart, taking with them a largely undeserved part of the supply of wealth. That wealth is, of course, still generated through the efforts of the entire social

54. *Improved communications, and especially the motor-driven private vehicle, make possible the move to low-density residential districts. Of course, this kind of scattered development is only possible with automobiles, and it necessitates a mobilization of wealth which can only be qualified as colonial, i.e., the use of natural resources of space and energy for private, individual benefit rather than for public, collective needs.* Los Angeles 'Free'-ways.

complex. It does not seem that the move away from the city, in western countries, can reasonably be said to represent the aspirations of a society, but only those of a certain social class. However, the entire society is required to subsidize that move, and a large and increasing part of the tangible social product, and of newly exploited natural resources, is appropriated to support it. Before we could say that such a movement represented the real aspirations of 'western' man and his societies, we would need to determine and to demonstrate clearly to him the social and economic costs which are entailed. This has never been done. The move has been more in the nature of a kind of gold rush to new real estate (property always appreciates, somehow) and/or a flight from society and responsibility.

55. *The old urban middle class is on the move, scattering itself to, and beyond, the fringes of the city, while the less fortunate (less wealthy) gravitate toward the center ... There is money to be made in the suburbs where new land can be 'improved' with building and resold at great profit.* Halen development outside Berne.

But cities are not dying, although they are deteriorating physically. They continue to be full of citizens, the new men, and they continue to be the locus of wealth, as well as the supporting structure of exchange – the exchange of goods and services, of ideas and methods. They also remain the treasuries of past history, and although what is past is necessarily obsolete, it is still human history and therefore vitally important to our heritage. These treasuries are not to be considered lightly since they contain vast resources in an inspirational sense for our continuing fight to humanize the urban environment.

We cannot disregard the cities on the assumption that they have gone out of style for a certain class. We might better say that that certain class itself has gone out of style, choosing to retreat from the city to a fictitious countryside. They will in all likelihood again become our associates as their dream evaporates and nature, which they destroy by embracing too closely, disappears.

For the moment, our efforts should be directed toward remaking a habitable human environment, out of the existing foundations as well as the new technologies. We need desperately to make a place for the citizen, a place which can be his, i.e. which he can appropriate and in which he need not feel either alienated or oppressed, and also a place which relates to his past in a meaningful way. To suburban expansion, we would reply with urban renovation. Suburban life is a chimera for most city dwellers; it cannot be held up as an ideal, since it clearly is not. Its only 'virtue' lies in its exclusivity, wherein lie also its most serious disadvantages.

But what can we do about the city, and its disfavored inhabitants? To suggest that we can do something is a great step forward, but obviously that is not enough. It will help to say that, in our sprawling societies, citizens (denizens of cities) have rights which are not less than those of sub- or ex-urbanites. It is sad to be obliged to state such an obvious truth but it is salutary to affirm it. Leftist opportunism, which feeds on every inequity, would find it preferable to see the urban situation continue to deteriorate, for only, so the dogma goes, out of total chaos can a new order be born. This is an unbelievably inhuman notion, and for that reason we must reject it. We may

56. *But cities are not dying, even though they deteriorate physically. They continue to be full of citizens, the new men, and they continue to be the locus of wealth as well as the supporting structure of exchange.* Fête in a covered street in the city of Santiago de Cuba.

believe that the old order will collapse under the weight of its own internal contradictions, but we cannot, because of that belief, encourage the proliferation of those contradictions. That is, indeed, a one-dimensional argument, and what viable new order would be born of such an inhuman abstraction is only subject to speculation. That 'pie in the sky' might well prove to be inedible.

We would then first seek to affirm the rights of the city and its citizens to an equitable part of the national pie. In our democracies such a position should be relatively easy to establish. Indeed in the last century many countries in Europe, and France first among them, have fought for parity in the other direction, holding that the capital cities were taking much too great a share. The movement need only be reversed, or stopped, or redirected. Our political systems are presumably responsive enough to balance these opposing forces, once sufficient light has been cast to illuminate the real situation. That situation is now clearly unfavorable to urban development and especially to urban redevelopment. The economic and financial forces of western capitalism – an adequate system in the past, perhaps – are clearly out of control. Expansionary economics can only operate by exploiting new resources, and space is not the least of these. In the irresponsible game of waste, the past investments are written off, dismissed by the state, and left unprotected while new short-term, high-profit investment is encouraged. Land, for instance, especially if it is undeveloped, is considered as being almost in the same category as consumer goods. In the same way that we no longer repair or maintain machines or other consumer goods, but simply throw them away when they no longer function properly, we are now beginning perhaps to think of cities as disposable rather than as being durable, maintainable, repairable. We urgently need to reconsider this position and to remember that the natural resource of open space is not an inexhaustible commodity which can be replaced. When it is used up, it is gone. We can ill afford, on the other hand, to neglect so wantonly our artificial patrimony, the massive investment which is represented by cities and their systems, the urban underground as well as the buildings, to the benefit of small numbers of land speculators who do not even know what to do with their gains, and, who, finally, become the victims of an outmoded, self-inflicted entrepreneurism. We have these cities, marvelous machines which are somewhat out of whack. They can be repaired and no doubt they will be repaired ultimately. However it is well to recall the city machine has worked best when it operated in tandem with the country non-machine. The city machine can only fall into greater disrepair if it is not only not repaired but is obliged to operate in a context from which it cannot draw any sustenance. This condition is now diligently being created out of national policy, or lack of policy, in most countries of the west. Not only is the city neglected in itself but the necessary nutrient environment in which it thrives, its countryside, is being denatured and even poisoned. The city cannot endure in an environment in which life itself dies.

The affirmation of the right of the city to live is tantamount to saying that the citizen has a right to a liveable environment, an obvious truth in which no one seems to believe. We shall return to this question in later parts of this book. It is sufficient now to say that, even while considering the renovation of the city, we cannot isolate it from its context which is regional, national, continental and global.

The machine is out of whack, more or less according to each case. It needs repair; it needs to be retuned to accommodate its new population, as well as what remains of its old population. We distinguish the new from the old, as they distinguish themselves from each other. The urbanist does not create categories of citizens; society does that, and he must begin by accepting those distinctions, but continue by examining their validity. We will go nowhere by pretending that they don't exist. The old burgher and the new citizen feel themselves to be different from each other, and this differential is a source of energy in itself. The business of the urbanist is to measure that energy and to use it economically in order to effect the changes which he clearly sees to be necessary. If that increment of energy is not channeled and controlled, it goes out of control and produces chaos. If it is inhibited, it bursts out in uncontrollable manifestations which are always, in every way, unproductive, or even destructive. It can be wasted, but not ignored. Change is inevitable in the city, but without constant elements, change in itself is meaningless. Recognizing and apprehending the energy potential which is generated by the desire for change, and by the gap between the old and the new, does not mean that the business of the urbanist is to set new against old, and thus to increase the potential. It means that he can discover in that accumulation of repressed energy a source of power which he can, and naturally will, use. We hope he will use it to a good end, and we may even be confident that he will, at first. But the truism about the corrupting influence of power on men still holds, and this power, if used demagogically, will absolutely corrupt the urbanist. Then this recognition of a source of power could degenerate into another kind of opportunism. The opportunism of the urbanist could be, and probably would be, an opportunism of the right, as opposed to the *laissez-aller* opportunism of the left which was mentioned earlier. The urbanist can hold within his hands a great deal of power. In general he is operating within a discipline which must appear to most people to be somewhat mysterious, if at times comical. Scratch an urbanist and you will find a mixture of good intentions, fraud, opportunism and all the other qualities which Machiavelli ascribed to the good prince. We are not very different from that prince of four centuries ago. We need, and use, the same crafts and wiles as he. It is never good enough to simply announce one's good intentions and then to expect them to be recognized and supported by either the authorities or the populace. Part of the populace (the old burghers) and therefore part of the authority (their representatives) will always be opposed and will see those good intentions as bad intentions. This is a normal state of affairs and it explains why the urbanist, in spite of his good intentions (a better world for every person on earth) often finds himself, because he put himself there, on the side of the forces of reaction, i.e. the forces which are opposed to change. Failing that, he tends to put himself in the forefront of the progressive camp and that action is usually fatally ineffectual. An urbanist must consider himself both as an agent for change and a guardian of constancy. By his discipline and his knowledge he must constantly be involved in the balancing of those opposing forces. He cannot simply say that the past should be eliminated because we have a new man and a new world. No more can he say that the *status quo* must be preserved because we are still living with the considerable investment which the old world has left to us.

Change is ineluctable, it is the essential expression of life. It will not obey laws of reason and logic. It has its own laws, just as molecular activity has, and they are overriding. Change will take place, no matter what barriers we erect against it. It is a natural phenomenon. But constancy, the desire and the need to not change, is a human characteristic. Almost all men, at almost every point in their history, have expressed this profound desire to fight change. The dynamics of this fight are what we perceive in our discipline as urbanism. We must, and will change something but we will quite rightly refuse to change everything. In this respect the urbanist is no more a king than the kings were, no more a revolutionary than Lenin, Mao or Castro. Nor is he less than a king or a revolutionary. In his recognition of the need for change, he will always be held back by his awareness of the desire to conserve what exists. In his conservatism he will always be stimulated by the pressing need for some change, even if only to keep the old systems alive. We do not feel that old systems, of finance or government, need necessarily be perpetuated but we recognize that a total change is unlikely, and, given the complexity of human relationships, may even be undesirable. To change this we must change that, but also to conserve this we must conserve that. There are surely many valuable qualities in our cities which we would wish to preserve. There are pernicious inequities which we would wish to abolish. In the balance between progress and stagnation, the urbanist will usually opt for progress. In the struggle between change and constancy, he will be circumspect. We are all subject to the natural law of change and we are all governed by the human law of constancy.

What can this mean, in cities of the west? Several interpretations are possible and probably all of them are equally false. Reference was made earlier to the complexity of human motivation in mass population movements, for instance, toward urbanization. We feel that such motive forces are not simple and cannot be reduced to a simple logic which we can easily comprehend. Above and beyond and behind the quantifiable, historically accurate, facts there lurks a horde of imponderables. We do not feel that we can describe, even with today's perspective, the entire range of motives which led man to the city. How much more difficult it would be to predict the future of man's relationship with his city, which is perhaps his greatest (or least) work, having no historical perspective save that which our computers can provide, and that is little or none. We can only speculate, since our complex man-made environment contains a multitude of cumulative actions, facts, attitudes, oppressions and resentments, the consequences of which we can never predict. One man's tax haven may be another man's hell. It is impossible to judge in advance the effect which a seemingly minor accommodation in the tax laws might produce upon the whole of the environment. Entire cities might be rehabilitated through such invisible devices, or they might be destroyed by changing a few words in the law which nobody reads before it is voted by parliaments who are said to represent the people.

Urbanists can only propose. They can propose what might be done, or what should be done, in order to rehabilitate rather than to destroy. We have these cities; they are ours, in direct succession to our fathers and grandfathers. We do not think that our considerable patrimonies should be dilapidated, in favor of suburban land speculation of the most sordid and cynical kind, or indeed of speculation of any kind. The force of our opinion comes from the fact of solidarity with all men on earth. We now realize that what happens in France happens to Chad; what happens in America happens to Peru. Our thinking, as western urbanists, has changed and we are faced with the global conscience which our grandfathers ignored. It is not a question of the 'white man's burden' but a question of the white man's conscience, and his recognition of the fact that he is no more important than the brown, black, yellow or red man. What urbanists do reflects this new attitude. We can propose many solutions to the problems of the white man's cities, but it is clear that none of these can reasonably rest upon the continuation of a theory of racial supremacy. The world does not owe us a living and we can no longer say that we may take whatever we can in order to support a ridiculously affluent and wasteful way of life for a certain class.

What then, do we do? I would suggest that, in the light of the above discussion, we once again place the city in its regional context, and in its global and continental context, consider its advantages and disadvantages – in reality and not in the myths propagated by urban or suburban land speculators – and judge with a cold and clear eye what should be done to make it a fit place for people, i.e. parents and children, to live.

What does the city need from us? First of all, it needs knowledge about what it needs. In the past urbanists have been reticent to proffer that knowledge, arguing that that was perhaps not their field. But then we may ask in all humility, what is their field? My 'field' as an urbanist is the knowledge of what the city needs. It is up to me to discover and to communicate that knowledge. Otherwise I am useless; I cannot speak with the citizens. Outside of knowledge there are only matters of taste. I would not deny the importance of such matters; I would only say that taste, or style, must be founded in knowledge. We can always hide our inadequacies behind questions of popular taste, e.g. 'the people don't want that' or 'the people want this,' but how can we know what the people want, and who are the people? If it is so easy to deal with the question as to condense it for a popularity poll, we may feel fairly certain that the question has not been well put. Inadvertently perhaps, the people have been misled into announcing a decision about a subject on which they have not been adequately informed. In any case, popular consultation is a dubious technique, at least in today's state of the art. What works for soap, or detergents, may not work equally well for the environment. It is extraordinarily difficult to extract any real knowledge, i.e. knowledge with which one may work, from a popular consultation. With what, then, may one work?

We work with our heads, i.e. our experience and historical knowledge of urban evolution as well as what we can glean from the behavioral sciences; and we work with our hearts, i.e. with our concern, one might say our enlightened concern, for the citizen and his life style. We do not have a great deal of influence over the quality of life, which depends largely or entirely upon the resources made available in any given situation, but given those resources we must see that they are employed most effectively in terms of that tentative life style. It is clearly inappropriate and absurd to propose a chateau life for all when we do not have at hand the resources to build the chateaux. One might object that the resources should be made available to build every man a chateau but this overruns the borders of demagogy, since such a deployment of wealth and building would be anti-economical in terms of infrastructure and equipment and would only exaggerate the global disparity of allocation of resources. We must, then, seek alternatives which are not only economical, in the best sense of the word, but which also correspond most closely with what we can know of the aspirations of the people toward a style of life which is harmonious with their urban situation.

The best sense of the word economical is of course that which is entirely consonant with the life of man in a given environment. Economical and ecological are parts of the same attitude, just as they are extracted from a common root. Any urbanism or architecture which is anti-economical will be perforce anti-ecological. Conversely any urbanistic or architectural decisions which tend to upset the ecological balance will necessarily prove to be anti-economical, even though they might produce short-term financial benefits to their authors. There is an enormous difference between economy and finance. The two are sometimes confused but it is important for the urbanist to see the difference. Finance is manipulation and management of money, while economy is the husbanding of the society's resources. Finance is profit-oriented, economy is survival. We have often seen financially profitable actions, such as war, which are economically disastrous.

With our heads and with our hearts, i.e. with strategic and normative inputs, with what we know is possible and with what we know to be desirable, we plot the destiny of urban man. Fortunately, we do not work in a vacuum; we are in constant contact with the man in question, in his many human manifestations. We can sound out his aspirations and show how they might be reconciled with his possibilities, his potential power. The man in the street, the man in his own man-made environment, is the essential resource of modern urbanism. 'No more second-hand God,' said Buckminster Fuller, and so saying he laid to rest the myth of Renaissance Architecture which was also urbanism. Renaissance in the suburb is not second- but third-hand God, and does not concern us in the least. Capital A Architecture and capital U Urbanism are safely things of the past, among our souvenirs. Small a and small u are our concern. And yet we have, among architects and urbanists, a nostalgia for that past, when we decided, on some basis of mystification, such as aesthetic judgement, just what was good for the people and for their tyrants.

Those were, essentially matters of taste (good or bad) which surrounded and stifled much simpler matters of organization. The king was in his counting-house, counting up the money. The counting-house is still with us but the king therein is no king at all, although we have done our best to make him appear a king. He has no responsibility, but only the meager authority of money, which can be overthrown at any time. His counting-houses are a basic part of the financial structure of cities, but he himself, at the center of gravity of all that money, is now invisible and anonymous. The architecture appropriate to the banker is on display in such buildings as the Chase Manhattan Plaza, in New York.

The behavioral sciences can tell us something of what people (our ultimate clients) really want and need. Unfortunately those sciences seem to be in a state very nearly as disarranged as the behavioral arts of architecture and urbanism. A time was when architects and urbanists thought they could pronounce with authority upon the needs and desires of the people. More recently they have oscillated between hard-line pronouncements and a certain incertitude. The hard-line pronouncements, in eastern Europe, for instance, led straight as an arrow to manipulative sociology, in which the client is made to fit the plan. Incertitude leaves most questions of fact up in the air, where perhaps they should be left for the present, in the absence of substantial evidence. We simply cannot determine to any useful degree the relationship between behavioral science and urbanism, or at least between the findings of the one and the programming of the other. All of our findings seem to be based upon situations which we have resolved to change radically. The description of life in a slum is of very little use as a program to someone who is resolved to eliminate slums. Of what use to him is a catalogue of misfortune when his entire effort is directed toward the eradication of the physical manifestations of that misfortune? The risk of perpetuating an instantaneous folklore of oppression is grave, when we strive to inform our plans with socio-historical input from observation; no self-respecting, or person-respecting, urbanist could follow such a road for long. We would seek to provide a decent habitat for the children of Sánchez,* not to conserve them in the trappings of their misery, like flies in amber, for our own intellectual delectation. Any attempt to transfer the admittedly magnificent *ad hoc* responses, which they have contrived in order to combat their oppressive environment, into a purportedly better future would be a risky business indeed.

However, we can make some observations about the nuclear family and the extended family, and we can build into our urbanism and architecture the possibility of accommodating these forms of association, without necessarily incorporating them as constraints. This means that we would seek to admit them without imposing them, that we would try to make an organization which can remain open to these or to other possible forms of association. In short, the input of information from sociological research to architectural or urban design is almost always a possible case, and rarely a positive direction. Urbanistic and architectural decisions still must come out of the architect's or urbanist's deep involvement with his subject, i.e. the city and its people, and their evolving life-style. Do we wish to perpetrate Bogside (Belfast), or Harlem (New York), or la Goutte d'Or (Paris), to build misery into the future? We would say not, but then what alternative will we propose? All populous slum quarters of all cities have secreted out of their miserable conditions certain unquestionable social benefits. To conserve these do we need to preserve their oppressive contexts? We don't think that the question can be put in this way. Rather we should ask ourselves what can we do so as not to destroy prematurely what we perceive to be the minimal and temporary advantages of those disadvantaged persons. Any intervention of the architect or urbanist is bound to modify the social context and to change the style of life. Urbanism is never very discreet, except perhaps when it limits itself to the rehabilitation of existing structures. Rehabilitation is extremely difficult in most western cities, since it implies a decrease in density with substantial dislocation of people living in overcrowded, slum conditions. Living space has been subdivided in order to jam more people in. Rehabilitation, under most building and sanitary codes, means reassembling

* LEWIS, OSCAR, *The Children of Sánchez*, Random House, Inc. New York, 1969 and Penguin, 1964.

living space into larger units. At the end, one is left with some excess population, for whom new space must be provided. That means that even rehabilitation of existing structures cannot usually be very discreet, unless those structures should chance to be abandoned or largely uninhabited. If such is the case it can usually be shown that replacement by new construction is a better choice, both socially and economically, than rehabilitation of old, worn-out, used-up buildings.

Urbanism is not discreet. The changes which it imposes on the physical environment will unquestionably be reflected in social attitudes and habits. The new man, as he becomes increasingly conscious of his power and control, through political process, takes an increasing part in the shaping of his new city. He, not we, will fight the forces of reaction, of *status quo* anti-urbanism, and beat them when he understands the stakes. With our help he is learning that urbanism is not discreet, that it proceeds with a heavy hand, and at the same time he is learning to choose the moments and places where he should choose the heavy hand of urbanism and where the velvet glove of rehabilitation is more suitable.

To illustrate this discussion of the renovation of cities, we have chosen four recent proposals for Frankfurt, Paris, New York and Karlsruhe. Although they are of different degrees of intervention, of different sizes and intensities of development, we feel that they reveal nevertheless a consistent approach to the problem of what to do when the city begins to come apart and there is presented an opportunity to do something. It is unlikely that any of these proposals will be followed by any immediately tangible result. We feel that their value lies not only in their urban and architectural quality but also in their power to vitalize the debate and to encourage others to combat the bureaucratic sloth and administrative timidity which has been consistently instrumental in dehumanizing the urban environment.

Essentially, all four proposals show that it is not impossible, in physical terms, to reconsider the city as an integrated entity, to combine and mix urban activities, to suggest reasonable priorities for transport, to create urban places and spaces which can be pleasant as

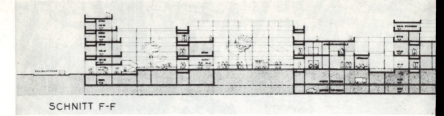

SCHNITT F-F

58. We proposed to accommodate all of the programmed development, and quite a lot more, in a low-rise, ground-scraper complex of four to five stories, based on a pedestrian-scaled grid of circulation and services. North–south section through Frankfurt city center. Levels below grade supply service, storage and parking areas. Natural light and ventilation are provided by interior courts, open to the sky. All roof areas are treated as terraces, accessible to public, or (where dwellings occur) private use. Fall in site allows bridging over road to reach river edge.

lorries and buses are accommodated beneath the complex in an underground servicing system.

The five-acre site would be entirely built over, to an average height of three stories, and the circulation system is a multi-level grid of pedestrian ways, mostly enclosed, interconnected vertically by escalators. These ways give access to various uses such as museums, galleries, shops, offices and dwellings at the different levels. In principle these pedestrian ways serve exactly the same function as a street in the city, except that they are not required to carry any traffic other than pedestrian. As in a city street, the uses and the building which accommodate them can change over time. Modern building techniques make possible the demounting and reutilization of practically all parts of the structure, which makes this scheme an ecologically and economically sound proposition. Natural light and ventilation, where needed, are provided by interior courts.

This scheme considers the center of the city as an entirely built environment, pedestrian-oriented and multi-storied, a layered web of open, covered or enclosed ways serving a mixed-use building. The city is considered as a building and the scheme demonstrates one way in which it might be organized. Such a development would, of course,

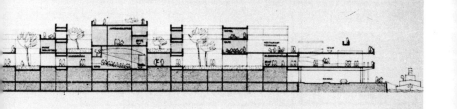

59. *To recreate the city scale within a totally modern structure, to live with both the past and the future on good terms.* Plan of proposed new development of Frankfurt city center, at ground floor level. (Architects: Candilis, Josic and Woods with Schiedhelm and Barp.) The area within the dotted lines contains the proposed new construction. A variety of uses are served by the public circulation system (shaded) which is sometimes open, sometimes covered, sometimes enclosed. This complex building is conceived so that the uses, and the structure which accommodates them, can change over time.

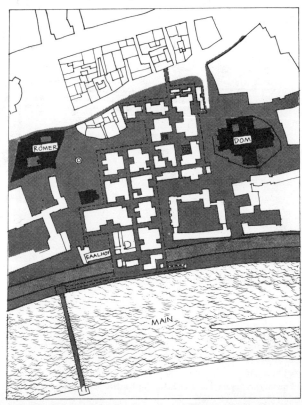

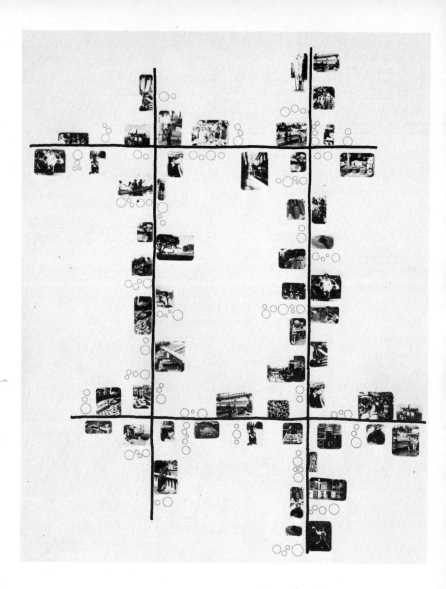

60. *The underlying principal of the scheme was an extremely simple grid of pedestrian ways to which correspond a servicing system, very like the street system which exists in most cities.* Web of activities, served by a grid of ways and serving multi-use construction. Basis for the Frankfurt renewal scheme, and later for Karlsruhe renovation.

61. *The circulation system is a multi-level grid of pedestrian ways, mostly enclosed, interconnected vertically by escalators.* The web used as an organizing device for a multi-storey building. (See also illustration no. 11, p. 25.) The idea is that public rights-of-way, at several levels, can be built into multi-use, multi-level buildings. They also correspond to the 3-d lattice of piped and wired mechanical services. These rights-of-way need not be superimposed; they could occur anywhere, but at present it is probably simpler, both legally and technically, to stack one above the other.

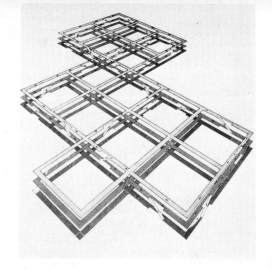

62. Second level of proposed new city center for Frankfurt. Public space is indicated by shading. Programmed uses included offices, educational and cultural facilities, entertainment and commerce. Residential use was also proposed to complete this program.

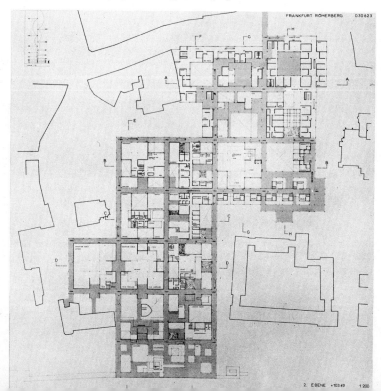

63. Cut-away model of part of the proposed new city center in Frankfurt. We would let those things which need to be complex develop their complexity around simple supporting systems of circulation, construction and mechanical services.

64. *This scheme considers the center of the city as an entirely built environment, pedestrian-oriented and multi-storied, a layered web of open, covered or enclosed ways, which serves a mixed-use building.* Model of proposed new city center for Frankfurt. View looking east, from the Town Hall to the Cathedral. Open space in front of Town Hall is preserved (see illustration no. 57, p. 123), while relationship of Cathedral to surrounding construction is re-established. The new world can live comfortably with the remnants and landmarks of the old, being neither subservient nor aggressive.

require some revision of existing laws governing public and private property, but the law is essentially reactive and enough precedents exist to cover most of the cases involved here. Obviously the scheme would work best if it were all in public ownership. We believe that this is not an unusual proposal, or even an unlikely one. The ground upon which the city is built belongs, finally, to the citizens, not individually, but in community.

Paris – Bonne Nouvelle

In a similar vein we studied the case of the center of Paris, when the central wholesale markets were removed to the edge of the urban agglomeration. This had the effect not only of liberating several acres occupied previously by the markets (splendid buildings which are unfortunately being demolished) but also of creating vacancies in the apartment buildings around the markets, where residential use had been displaced by commercial use connected with the markets. We reasoned that this decongestion could provide an occasion to begin an urban renewal operation in the crowded slums immediately north of the markets, the Bonne Nouvelle quarter.

A plan was produced, showing how this quarter could be renewed and reorganized, again as a pedestrian-oriented sector of the city center. The proposal was to proceed by stages, relocating the existing population into new buildings as the scheme proceeded. The number of dwellings built would eventually accommodate the present population in this densely settled quarter.

The plan is based on a web of pedestrian circulation, taking the form of glassed-over arcades, which connect to points on the metropolitan transit systems – Métro and buses. This arcaded street system provides access to mixed-use buildings, about ten stories high, in which office floors alternate with residential floors. Vertical circulation systems are independent for each use, so as to reduce potential conflict. Educational, social, cultural and commercial ancillaries are located at the lower levels principally, along the street system. A separate road system for servicing is provided. The change

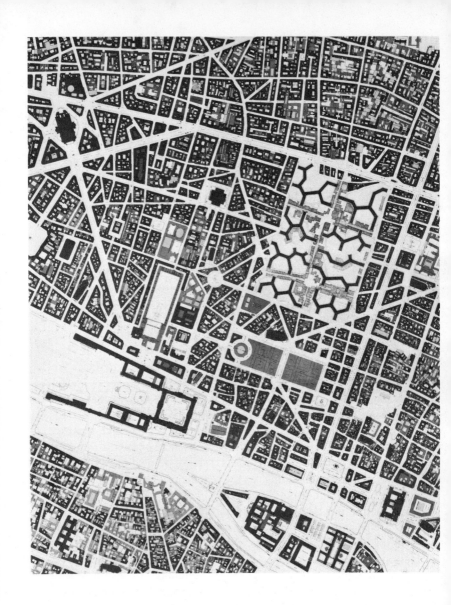

65. *An occasion to begin an urban renewal operation in the crowded slums immediately north of the markets, the Bonne Nouvelle quarter. A plan was produced showing how this quarter could be renewed and reorganized as a pedestrian-orientated sector of the city center.* Example of how the Bonne Nouvelle quarter might be renewed. Darkest shading shows lower buildings containing ancillaries. Central markets (les Halles) are south of Bonne Nouvelle. (Architects: Woods with Pfeufer.)

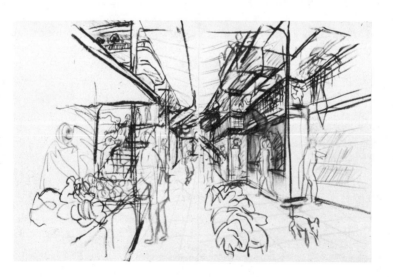

66. Bonne Nouvelle, mixed-use buildings plugged into arcaded stem of ancillaries. Both office and residential use are accommodated in the high-rise buildings, with deeper office floors providing terraces for maisonnettes above them.

67. *The plan is based on a web of pedestrian circulation, taking the form of glassed-over arcades, which connect to points on the metropolitan transit systems.* Drawing of arcade with shops. As the drawing suggests the arcaded pedestrian street system might be completed with a mini-rail overhead transit system.

in scale, from the existing five to six story buildings, to ten story is not overwhelming, and considerable open space is gained. The ground, except for the service roads, is given over entirely to the pedestrian. No parking is provided, since none is needed, and we feel certain that it is a grievous error to encourage private ownership of automobiles in a city well-endowed with public transportation systems. The layering of office and residential uses has many advantages, among which are: twenty-four hour use of mechanical systems, vertical privacy between residential floors (especially appreciated at night) and integration of urban activities with reduction of peak loading of transport facilities. In addition, this place in the city is one where people can at least see what others do, and ideally could meet and exchange views and opinions. We feel that this is especially important for the children of the city and their parents and teachers, although it is probably important for the office workers, too, not to be exiled daily to the 9 a.m. to 5 p.m. mines, where nothing blooms but bureaucracy. It is an effort to humanize the city.

68. *The arcaded street system provides access to mixed-use buildings, about ten stories high, in which office floors alternate with residential floors. Vertical circulation systems are independent for each use. Educational, social, cultural and commercial facilities are located at lower levels.* Ideogram of Bonne Nouvelle scheme, showing mix of activities extending throughout the complex of buildings.

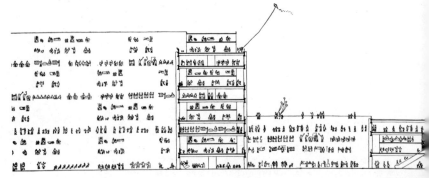

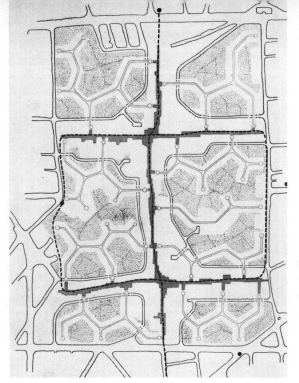

69. Abstract from plan for Bonne Nouvelle showing principal pedestrian stem in dark gray, public or semi-public open spaces in light gray. A possible circuit of mini-rail type public transportation is indicated by the dashed line. It can be seen that no provision is made for car-parking and that service ways are kept to an absolute minimum (it is assumed that loading facilities will be built-in to those buildings which require them).

70. A typical arcaded shopping street in Paris, near the Bonne Nouvelle quarter. Such *passages* are traditional in parts of Paris, like the second *arrondissement*. We have tried to incorporate that tradition of protected pedestrian streets in the scheme for Bonne Nouvelle, without packing so densely the development which lies behind these arcades.

Manhattan – SoHo

A similar effort was proposed in our study of a part of the lower Manhattan manufacturing district, called SoHo because it lies south of Houston Street. Here again, problems of congestion, scale and use were present but an additional and important factor was the architec-

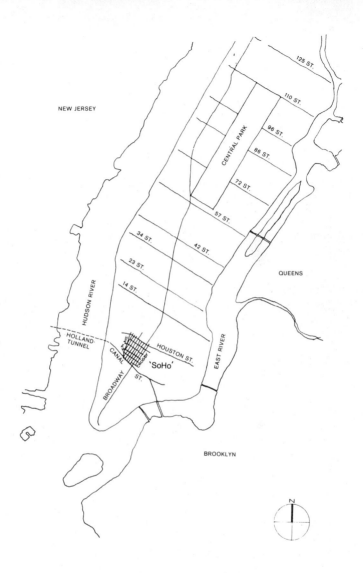

71. *A part of the lower Manhattan manufacturing district, called SoHo because it lies south of Houston Street.* Buildings in the area are generally about one hundred years old with no off-street loading facilities and cramped spaces (many on 25 × 100 foot lots). However, the skilled and semi-skilled jobs in the manufacturing district form an important part of the city's economic base (about 120,000 jobs, of which around 25,000 in the thirty-two blocks of SoHo). It is considered essential to the city to conserve these jobs in this central location.

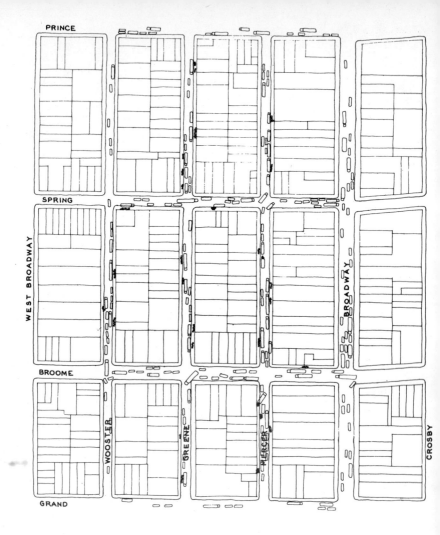

72. *Streets planned for horse-drawn vehicles do not easily accommodate sixty-foot semi-trailers.* Partial plan of SoHo area, showing
congestion of traffic caused by use of the public streets as loading and
delivery zones. Blocks and buildings are too small for any corrective
action to be contemplated. Through traffic on east–west streets is
impeded by back-up of delivery traffic on north–south streets. The
situation has a strangling effect on manufacturing activities (which are
vital to the city's economic base), and can only be relieved by reorder-
ing the traffic patterns and loading areas.

tural quality of some of the existing loft buildings with their handsome cast-iron fronts.

SoHo has been deteriorating largely because the spaces available for light manufacturing are cramped and ill-equipped, and the streets are narrow and congested. Streets planned for horse-drawn vehicles do not easily accommodate sixty-foot semi-trailers.

We proposed to reorganize the street pattern by closing half the streets, to accommodate the heavy servicing by taking the lorries off the streets and into new buildings with loading facilities serving freight elevators to the manufacturing floors, to conserve the best of the cast-iron buildings as frontage on the new lofts, converting them into offices or other uses (e.g. *galeries* or *ateliers* for artists) where they were too small to accommodate industrial operations, and to add residential use above the new loft buildings with the roofs of the new five-story lofts serving as recreational, community and educational space for the dwellings.

This is again an attempt to demonstrate the possibilities of mixed use development of the urban fabric. No incompatibility exists between the light manufacturing uses which concentrate in this quarter (printing, garment-making, electronics, etc.) and residential use. In fact, as the existing loft buildings are vacated by manufacturers seeking more space and better servicing (both of which we would provide in this scheme) they are being converted clandestinely to residential and work use by artists. This operation is clandestine because New York's zoning ordinances prohibit new dwellings in manufacturing zones. Our proposal assumes that the zoning ordinances will be revised, not a very difficult process since zoning, like law, is always responsive to public pressure. SoHo would then be reintegrated into the city with manufacturing, commercial and residential uses contiguous but not conflicting. This could, we are sure, only rebound to the benefit of workers and residents, and to the city as a whole, in the same ways that the Bonne Nouvelle proposal would in Paris.

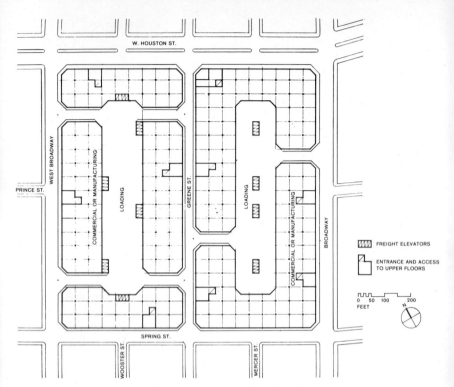

73. Ground floor plan showing theoretical regrouping of small 200′ × 400′ blocks into super blocks completely covered by loft buildings. This is done by closing alternate streets, both north–south and east–west. Loading activities are removed from the remaining streets to the interior of the new super block, whence distribution takes place by large-capacity freight elevators to both upper and lower floors. Remaining streets are adequate for circulation and are limited to circulation (moving vehicles).

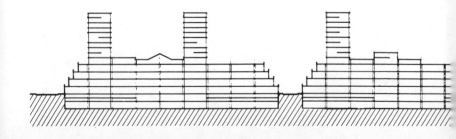

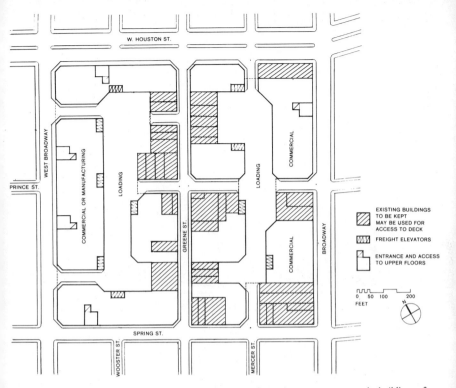

74. Adaptation of ground floor plan to preserve certain buildings of undisputed architectural value (mostly cast-iron fronts dating from the 1860s–1870s). The principle of off-street loading is preserved, and it is proposed that the remaining old buildings be used for small scale activities, such as offices, galleries, artists' or artisans' studios, etc. Some of this activity has already moved into this area and could be encouraged to remain.

DWELLINGS

COMMUNITY

LOFTS

SHOPS
PARKING
STORAGE

75. Section through new super block loft building showing how dwellings might be built above the new manufacturing spaces, using their roof as a new 'ground plane' for ancillary activities, community facilities, schools and playgrounds. In this way a desirable mix of residential and light industrial use might be established. This mix is already trying to establish itself, in total chaos, in the SoHo area.

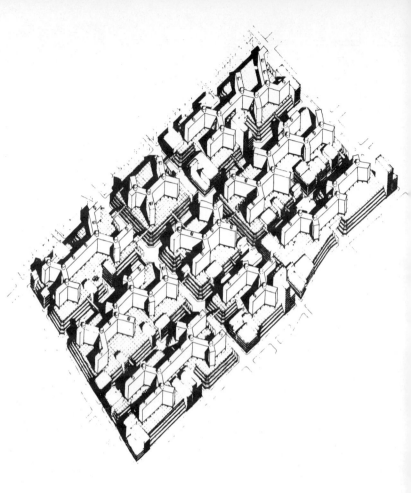

76. *This is again an attempt to demonstrate the possibilities of mixed-use development of the urban fabric.* Sketch showing how the ideas presented above might be extended to the entire SoHo area, forming a well-serviced layer of manufacturing space, on which is superimposed a system of dwellings. The geometry of the residential buildings is at this stage schematic, intending merely to indicate a density, and to show how conditions of overlooking and over-shadowing can be optimized in continuous buildings.

77. *In Karlsruhe, in Germany, an urban renewal scheme was put forth to replace the most insalubrious quarters of this Baroque city.* Aerial view of Karlsruhe from the south-east. The quarters to be renewed, where work has already begun on a new dual-carriageway, lie in the south-east quadrant.

Karlsruhe

In Karlsruhe, in Germany, an urban renewal scheme was put forth to replace the most insalubrious quarters of this Baroque city, and an architectural competition was held to determine the new urban form. Here again we proposed to limit the access of the private automobile toward the center, restricting it to peripheral parking garages linked to the main arterial road system. Buildings of mixed use are organized around vast interior gardens and are served by a grid of pedestrian ways which are also accessible to service vehicles. A scale compatible with the existing Baroque buildings is proposed. Educational, cultural, commercial and residential uses are included within the buildings unselfconsciously. The ground level is given over to pedestrianized public use, and the first floor above ground

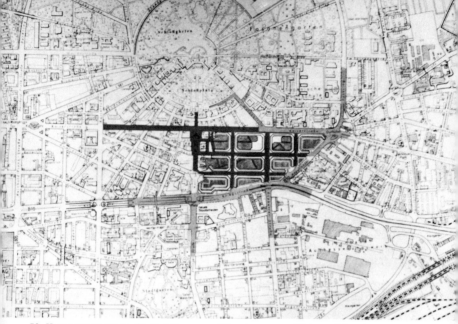

78. *Here again we proposed to limit the access of the private automobile toward the center.* Karlsruhe, streets reserved to pedestrian and service access are indicated in dark gray.

79. *Buildings of mixed-use are organized around vast interior gardens and are served by a grid of pedestrian ways which are also accessible to service vehicles.* Karlsruhe, proposed building organization.

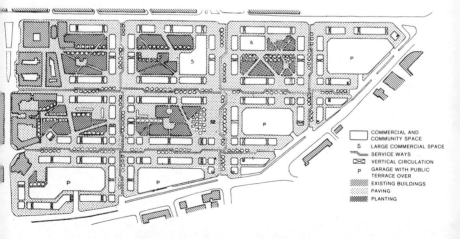

COMMERCIAL AND COMMUNITY SPACE

S LARGE COMMERCIAL SPACE

SERVICE WAYS

VERTICAL CIRCULATION

P GARAGE WITH PUBLIC TERRACE OVER

EXISTING BUILDINGS

PAVING

PLANTING

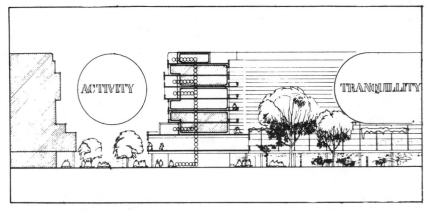

80. *This plan is an attempt to demonstrate the possibility of a new style of in-town living, with street-oriented activities and garden-oriented tranquillities coexistent.* Karlsruhe, activity and tranquillity.

81. Karlsruhe, existing street pattern. The radials extending the original plan, which stopped at Kaiserstrasse, the principle east–west thoroughfare, have only a tenuous relationship to the former place, today a museum.

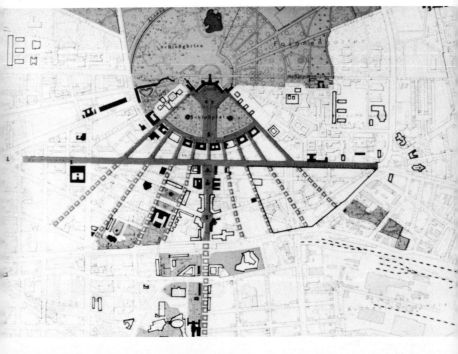

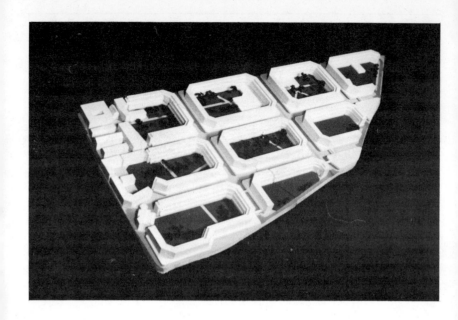

82. *It does, however, propose to live comfortably with the Baroque remains, while revealing a new, open system of planning.* Karlsruhe model.

83. *Appropriate urban space.* Karlsruhe perspective view toward Kaiserstrasse from one of the north–south streets. By excluding private cars the entire use of the ground is recovered for pedestrians. The morphology of the buildings insures a comprehensible circulation pattern.

also accommodates public and semi-public uses, including schools, day care centers, cultural and leisure uses.

Although this plan does not present the intensity of use of Frankfurt, Bonne Nouvelle and SoHo, it follows the same general line of reasoning. Karlsruhe is a city of 250,000, with a strong tendency to suburbanization. This plan is an attempt to demonstrate the possibility of generating a new style of in-town living, with street-oriented activities and garden-oriented tranquillities coexistent. It makes no attempt to extend the axes of the Baroque radial plan since these are tenuous and inefficient at this distance from the central Palace, which is today a museum. It does, however, propose to live comfortably in scale with the Baroque remains, while revealing a new, open system of planning, compatible with a contemporary citizen's ideas and comprehensible to him. He is not a second-hand king, nor a subject, but a man in need of appropriate urban space.

3. Growth of Cities

Cities not only change, they also grow. The process of urbanization in the western world has been accelerating in the past century, with population increases in urban areas far outstripping the general growth rate. Part of this increase is accommodated, after a fashion, by densification and renewal within the boundaries of the city, but much of it forces the city to extend its limits into the surrounding countryside, occupying more land. Thus cities grow in area as well as in population, and they generally grow in an undisciplined, disordered fashion, with the occupation of the lands around them being as much, or more, conditioned by arcane and usually irrelevant financial considerations as by 'urbanistic' criteria. Only rarely do we see a clearly defined policy of land use for the extension of the city, as was the case, for instance, of London's green belt.

Urban extension requires regional, and even national, planning if we are to avoid ecological and social disaster. We need to come to some conception of what may be the reasonable limits of urban growth and what alternate policies might be developed to accommodate the urban-attracted population as well as the natural increase. We need certainly to examine and evaluate the effects of unbridled growth, so that we may say whether or not we will continue to permit public areas to be appropriated for private gain, to the detriment of present and future societies.

All land that has not been built upon may be considered as part of the public domain, whether it is in private ownership or not. The act of building is a serious one, for it removes a part of the public (or potentially public) space. The parts removed are nearly impossible to restore or replace, since that would involve legal and financial support of a high order, such as the exercise of the right of eminent domain and the writing-off of investments in infrastructure and buildings. In view of these probable difficulties we can make the assumption that once land is 'improved' it is gone forever from the public domain. We can assert that the land, all of the land, belongs to the people, but when the people give up to private use any part of the land a system of inequitable use is established and the law, which is equally an instrument of social harmony, must protect the investment of that private user. In the totally built environment which we see our cities and countries to be, the question of land use, and land ownership, is surely the most perplexing one. When land, in the American idiom, is 'improved' by building upon it, the part that is built upon loses any potential for public ownership or use under existing law. It is easily seen that unless the building on that land is part of a planning program we cannot aspire to any reasonable planning for urban extension. However, since that land is an essential part of any planning intention we are unable to allow it to be used up indiscriminately. Every city, as a matter of survival, needs to be able to control land use in its environs.

The problem is an extremely complex and delicate one. On the one hand, we know today that growth is inevitable. We also know that growth probably means occupying previously unbuilt areas. On the other hand, our most basic human instincts demand that we preserve unbuilt areas not only for ourselves, but also for future generations – the future extensions of ourselves. The need for procreation is essential in all life. In man that need is associated with and tempered by the realization that procreation can only exist if we prepare a viable physical milieu in which future human life may develop. 'Where there's life, there's hope,' says the old proverb, but if there is only hope there may very well be no life.

The massive extension of cities has several origins: the industrial revolution attracting men from hard and uncertain work on the land to what seemed to be an easier and more secure life in the cities; the agricultural revolution requiring fewer and fewer people on the land, tending toward efficiency in the use of labor, reducing the percentage part of agriculture in the national product; the medical and scientific revolutions, which ensure population growth (increase of viable

84. *On one hand we know today that growth is inevitable. We know that growth probably means occupying previously unbuilt areas. On the other hand, our most basic human instincts demand that we preserve unbuilt areas, not only for ourselves but also for future generations.* Paris, Bois de Vincennes.

births over deaths) at the same time that they decrease the need for agriculture labor; the cultural and social revolution, which tends to make culture an urban product, available only in the cities, and to widen the gap between culture and agriculture, thereby relegating farm people to an inferior status; the financial revolution, which regards the product of human labor as inferior or inefficient, and favors investments in mysteriously important fields such as 'services,' governmental and corporate bureaucracy, research and development of tools whose use is questionable or problematic, tending again to expand the urban labor market; and finally, the need to exploit new resources, of which space near cities is at the present the most easily available and profitably exploitable.

As the population increases, and an ever greater part of the population gravitates to the cities, enormous problems of congestion and expansion are created. Overcrowding in cities and under-use of the space around the cities are two manifestations of an outworn attitude toward human society. *Laissez-faire* style free enterprise is admittedly an attractive philosophy but it has proven itself to be inadequate as a social and political policy in an increasingly urbanized world. It will probably continue to inflict its inadequacies on future generations unless it is restrained or abandoned. In North America today, administrations are 'experimenting' with government incentives to private industry in an attempt to resolve these problems, under the assumption that private capital, sufficiently subsidized, will demonstrate a greater efficiency than government management would. One may dispute this thesis seriously, on purely theoretical grounds. At a practical level, however, it resolves itself into a use of the tools which exist (private industry) through subsidies with virtually no control possible. The people must come, hat in hand as it were, to beg of the captains of industry that they undertake, for a handsome profit, to perform the function for which they exist. There is perhaps no other way, in the west. And if the job gets done, then we can only rejoice that at least there existed a system by which the people could pay those willing entrepreneurs to perform their tasks at 'cost plus . . .' It would seem, however, that the government could perform the same functions, more efficiently and more knowledgeably, by nationalizing the building industry and controlling more closely the allocation of funds and resources.

In any case, what needs to be done will unquestionably be done, and if we need to create a few more millionaires in the construction process, we could only regard that as a necessary evil. Where the evil becomes unnecessary, and pernicious, is in the planning and development processes. Although free enterprise in the construction of buildings may be questionable but considered generally as 'healthy,' the same free enterprise in planning is certain to be deadly, both to the existing city and to its environs, which are necessarily part of its ecology. Free enterprise cannot be reconciled with the idea of planning; they are incompatible. Free enterprise will always follow the line of least resistance, since it seeks maximum profits, whereas planning has to deal with choices that are based on other criteria. Should we leave the land around our cities to be developed freely, at the will of the entrepreneurs, we would soon see the most unintelligible, unimaginable, inefficient and disorganized sprawl of low-density development. This is, in fact, what we can observe, from Melbourne to Los Angeles to Berlin; wherever the option has been left open and the controls removed, or not established. There is an enormous waste of space and resources, to accommodate an infinitesimal part of the population. Worse, that part does not even share equitably in the cost of maintaining elaborate suburbs, which still depend upon the presence of the city for sustenance, both psychic and physical. We believe that it can be shown that the space-wasteful, energy-consuming, low-density suburb is veritably parasitic, not only in the sterilization of urban public land but also in the burdens which it inevitably must inflict upon the city, either through removal of a part of the tax base or through direct or indirect subsidy. The suburbanite, for instance, profits from all the resources of the city, from universities and hospitals, to work and leisure facilities. Rarely does he make any contribution to the financing of those ancillaries which are offered him. He depends upon the city, on its streets and services, on its administration; he lives off it but not in it. He pays his rates elsewhere.

For reasons which escape us, administrative boundaries are fixed arbitrarily, and the 'city limits' no longer mean the edges of the city, but only a change in local administration, which renders difficult, if not impossible, any reasonable operation of the entire urban complex. We should then perhaps choose to subdivide even further so the immediate community could exercise greater control over their physical and administrative environment. The question of size, the physical dimension of the community is undoubtedly of great importance. Administrative boundaries are generally of little significance to the people who live within them except when they act as effective barriers to the sensible operation of municipal services, or create tax anomalies between the citizens. It is clear that suburbs exist as a dependency of the city, and perhaps sometimes as a support for it. But to what extent can they be part of it? Are eccentric large scale developments parts of their parent cities? Is Sarcelles part of Paris, is the Märkisches Viertel part of Berlin, is Staten Island part of New York? For that matter, is anywhere a part of anything? Do Manhattan and Queens really work as reciprocating parts of a whole, or are they mutually destructive? Obviously the answer is that the one (Queens) could not exist without the other (Manhattan). But the questions which nag remain. Do we need to have Queens, or Brooklyn, or the Bronx, in order to have Manhattan? To pile up so much profitable commercial use in one place, was it necessary to destroy so much countryside? One feels that a national or regional policy of controlled development would have better resolved the problem.

We have arrived at a point where it is possible to think in terms of regional and national development policies, and our hope is that we no longer need to generate both congestion and sprawl in order to extend the life of the city. Staten Island, Sarcelles, or the Märkisches Viertel could be other cities, or at least the nuclei of other cities, if they had been thought of as such, rather than being considered simply as dormitories for the commuting workers of the central city.

It is clear that the extension of cities, under the pressures of urbanization and population growth, should be carefully considered. It may not be a very good idea simply to extend the residential city without extending and amplifying its basic structure and its services infrastructure. Since these things are measurable, especially the latter, we would be well-advised to weigh carefully the advantages and disadvantages of unlimited urban growth. In a world whose physical limits we have come to know intimately, we need desperately to adopt some policies for human settlement. Whereas we will probably never admit that humans – men, women, and children – must conform to an administrative policy of settlement, we must nevertheless seek how an increasingly urban population may best be accommodated. For our part, we see these alternatives: 1) densification and extension of existing cities, and 2) creation of new cities.

Both require very careful planning. It is impossible today to fix the limits of number for any city of the west. The capital cities, the 'great cities' have long since grown beyond any imaginable number. New York has some 8,000,000 inhabitants; London has 10,000,000; Paris has 6,000,000, etc. (give or take a million). It is possible to imagine the growth of these figures, today, to two or three times the present population, without any forseeable point of saturation being reached. We can achieve this through intelligent planning of the use

85. *The questions which nag remain: do we need to have Queens, Brooklyn or the Bronx in order to have Manhattan? To pile up so much profitable commercial use in one place, was it necessary to destroy so much countryside?* Manhattan seen from Queens.

of land and resources and communications. We could however, equally propose that additional development be concentrated in new settlements, outside of the existing centers, which would then only be renewed to accommodate their natural population growth. We could easily imagine an entirely new network of new cities, superimposed on the old network of existing cities.

We have learned that growth *per se* is costly. The growth of cities leads to congestion and an overloading of their essential services, both the urban underground (sewers, water, electricity, and gas supply, transport, etc.) and the above-ground services such as schools, police, fire-fighting, street-cleaning, parks and playgrounds, and distribution of goods throughout the extended city. Growth as an economic theory has been seriously attacked by reputable thinkers.* Growth as an urban theory might even be more shaky, given an alternative. An image of growth might be the pyramid: as the apex goes higher, the base extends and the center of gravity supports ever more weight. In the urban pyramid, the center must accommodate increasing congestion. But the center is usually the oldest part, the original nucleus, and thus the part least adaptable to the changes necessary to accommodate additional activities and movements. The center of gravity also represents the greatest mass of existing invest-ment, and therefore the part of the urban pyramid which will most resist change. Under these circumstances, the idea of continuous growth of existing cities tends to lose its attractiveness. Growth is perhaps inevitable but it must certainly be controllable. Cities will continue to extend themselves; we need to consider in what ways.

Any addition to the city is, or should be, an extension of the city. This means that the parts of the city must all extend simultaneously. By the parts we mean the entire structure of activities which give support to the life of the city. We cannot conceive of new additions in terms of strictly limited functional uses, such as residential, commer-cial, cultural, industrial or institutional uses. These might as well be called functional abuses, since such clear-cut definitions and zones

* See for example, MISHAN, E. J., *The Costs of Economic Growth*, International Publications Service, New York, 1970 and Penguin, 1969.

would constitute in fact an abuse of the city, whether they occur centrally or peripherally. Such concepts are based on a complete misunderstanding of what the nature and purpose of the city might be. They tend, in fact, to atomize the urban experience, to break it down into unintelligible components, to dissociate the parts rather than to associate them in a comprehensible whole. When land-use zoning becomes an objective of urbanism, we, the men in the street, can no longer apprehend or comprehend the new urban milieu. It then becomes strange to us, and we are alienated within it. As the city extends its physical, although not necessarily its administrative boundaries, we see an increasing dissociation of uses. The extensions are all residential or industrial, for instance, while tertiary commercial and institutional uses tend to displace other functions at the center. The city then becomes a disarticulated web of polarities, and few of us can make any sense of it.

With the pressures of natural growth plus immigration from rural areas, vast new tracts of land are being developed. Unfortunately the new development is usually of the most urgently short-sighted kind, i.e. residential use in low-density, high-profit patterns or in medium-density, low-profit, subsidized clumps. We need, of course, to house the people, but housing is not nearly enough. We need also to create a habitat for them, to establish relationships with their places of work and leisure, to make an urban place which they can appropriate for themselves, and with which they identify. Extensions of the city cannot be simply additions to it. Every citizen has the right to the city and to his own part of the city, and it must really be part of the city, not simply a detached, disinherited suburb, whose only relationship with the city is through a tenuous, often unhealthy, uninviting, unpleasant and inconvenient transit link. There are great possibilities in reversing the problem, and this is within the power of almost every

86. *Every citizen has the right to the city and to his own part of the city, and it must really be part of the city, not simply a detached, disinherited suburb, whose only relationship with the city is through a tenuous, often unhealthy, uninviting, unpleasant and inconvenient transit link.* Paris suburb, the commuter train before dawn.

city planning agency. Instead of increasing residential use at the edge, and concentrating other uses in the center, why not adopt a policy of mixed-use extension? The economic base should accompany residential use, and so should the cultural and institutional base, if the city is to be well-based. It makes no sense to continue, presumably, following trends which are artificially generated, to isolate the parts of the city one from the other, increasing the congestion and overloading of distribution and transportation systems, extending urban areas with no perceivable urban function, adding to the dissatisfaction of the urban population, making places in which life is lived on a part-time basis, aggravating environmental problems to the greater profit of automobile manufacturers, and generally creating an impossible world for our successors, as well as for ourselves.

It may be that these things are done simply because we have forgotten, or neglected, the alternative way of doing things. We must admit that urbanists are well-motivated. Their decisions, when they see any choice, are based on a way of thinking that has come to be generally accepted. Our difficulties arise from the fact that what is generally acceptable for the urbanist has very little relationship with the way people and cities, and people in cities, live, or wish to live. However, the reduction of all information to quantifiable fact has led us far astray. In this situation, what the urbanist knows is what gets printed out of the computer. This is very thin knowledge indeed, and comes from what can be programmed into the computer, i.e. out-of-date information on the ponderable aspects of human settlements and their functional interrelationships. The information is of necessity always out-of-date and the imponderables are always necessarily neglected. We have forgotten many things, in this process, and first among them is the simple fact that cities are for people, not against them, and certainly not for the convenience of the computer-driven urbanist. We will not question his motives, which are pure, but we will certainly question his decisions and tactics, which are repressive when they are detached from the human context, and rely solely on the half-truths which are the computer's binary province.

The recent history of the extension of cities of the west is instructive principally as a complete manual of errors; a missal of mistakes in which we can follow the consequences of wrong decisions, at every level of government and administration, on how to deal with the problems of increasing urbanization without offending any special-interest group of any power whatever. The offense is perpetrated, sometimes unwittingly, against the entire urban society, and of course especially against the ignorant and willing victims who dwell in the new 'functional' (i.e. use-zoned) single-class suburban areas. It is they, and their children, who suffer most from the unnatural isolation which they have so eagerly sought. Alienation in the suburbs has long been a favorite and fertile ground for social behaviorists to till. 'What is wrong with our children?' is the plaintive cry heard from all azimuths around (but far from) the city. The complaining parents cannot understand that the young should not entirely approve the choices which they so carefully made in moving their new families out of reach of the menace of the city's rich mix of classes and activities, and into the plastic image of happyland, away from life and change and into a sterilized, pre-packaged, full-color, stable and predictable world where each family has 2·5 children (one of each) running merrily across the surrounding privately-owned greensward. After all, it was all done for *them*; all the 'sacrifices,' all the saving and indebtedness, all the degrading boredom was endured so that they would have a better place in which to grow. And then, when all is done, each blade of grass in place, each dwelling completely equipped with enough consumer goods to render it desperately autonomous, the ungrateful young turn their backs on it all, and we discover that it was not so much that sacrifices were made for *them* but that they were sacrificed to their parents' ambitions for a representation of 'success' within their class. One cannot but think that it would be much more sane for the parents to choose (when they have a choice) their abode with more regard for their own needs and less attention to the images of happy childhood which are fabricated in advertising mills for popular consumption. Where the parents' needs are reasonably satisfied, the children have a better chance of being content, since they might then see some possible future pattern of integration into a reasonable adult world.

Bedroom suburbs, industrial 'parks,' 'shopping' centers (where one goes shopping, i.e. an activity without objective) office 'plazas' and 'campus' schools accessible only by motor, are all pieces of the anti-city. Semantic nostalgia has led some to call this disparate collection of parts the 'outer city' and thence to hail it as a new and exciting cultural advance. Advance it surely is not, except in strictly temporal terms, which would also qualify the Vietnam War as an advance over the Korean War. This kind of development around

87. *Bedroom suburbs, industrial 'park' 'shopping' centers, office 'plazas' and 'campus' schools ... are all pieces of the anti-city. Semantic nostalgia has led some to call this disparate collection of parts the 'outer city' and thence to hail it as a new and exciting cultural advance.* Shopping center in Huntington, Long Island, outside New York. Ineptly called the Walt Whitman shopping center, it does no honor to the poet.

cities might more aptly be described as a cancer of the city and its milieu, a disorganized proliferation of non-viable cells which inhibits and even destroys healthy development.

It can be said, however, that this cancerous growth is a direct expression of popular, middle-class demand, and that it sells and therefore is justified. Demographic surveys have always shown, in every western country, a distinct preference for the individual home, standing on its own ground. These surveys may prove only that foolish answers will always be given to foolish questions. The need and desire for roots, *l'enracinement* as Simone Weil called it, is probably a strong universal characteristic of industrialized western society. However, this does not necessarily imply a totally atomized, mutually antagonistic confrontation of non-urban entities. The setting apart of classes and races, as we have seen in North America, and the United States, especially, soon leads to social polarization and racism, and then escalates to sexism and generational confrontation (which might be called a kind of infantilism). The loss of social integration, which is one of the manifestations of suburban scatter, is everyone's loss.

We see clearly that the need for some policy of urban development, at suitable governmental levels, exists in most countries of the west. Free enterprise, uncontrolled, in the development and extension of urban areas, has naturally been more concerned with quick profits than with the long-range results of its hasty interventions. Sadly, we must note that the methods of the Adam brothers give quite different results when applied by Levitt and Sons. Levittown has nothing in common with the Adelphi, except free enterprise. The Adams' commitment to style and to the shape of the city, and their responsibility, have disappeared from the entrepreneur's set of attitudes. We are no longer making our cities good places to live, revalorizing land, as Le Corbusier called it; we are simply using up land in the worst possible way. In view of the irresponsible attitudes which are now held by the land 'developers,' the need for control, responsive to the needs of the citizens and their societies, has become evident.

We need then to plan for the extension of cities, and/or to plan new cities, to accommodate the growth of urban population. We need to be parsimonious, not profligate, with our decreasing resources of space. But we especially need to provide real urban environments, complex and integrated, complete and comprehensible, for those who choose or are forced to make the city their home. To provide for the growth of cities, or to create new ones, we need to consider not how to simplify matters by mindless classification and separation of uses and activities, but how to complicate matters which are, and need to be, complex. Urbanism has principally to do with life-support systems and the organization of human activities. It cannot pretend to any such simple-minded gestures as land-use zoning. When it does, it produces chaos, a caricature of urban life, segregated prisons designated with such artificial labels as 'white- or blue-collar,' 'low-, middle-, or high-income,' 'work,' 'commerce,' 'recreation,' and that most unreal of all tags: 'culture.' It is as though we would deny that all of these are part of each other and that all are part of the urban scene.

We would say that planning, urbanism, is quite the opposite of classification and segregation of activities into clearly identifiable zones. We would argue for integrating as much as possible all urban activities into all the parts of the city, and the extensions of the city. This does not mean that one would lump everything together in disorder, which might only create new and unsuspected conflicts. It does mean that an organic, adaptable form of organization should be sought, so that that entire spectrum of urban activities, in various constellations, can be accommodated within a comprehensible system. A comprehensible system is one that will not only serve various activities but also be understandable to the user, the citizen. He must be able to detect it in the relationship of the parts to the whole, and to each other. He must be able to find his way about in it, and to adapt it as necessary to his changing needs.

It may seem unfair and irrelevant to compare the Adam brothers to Levitt and Sons. While they lived in a developing city, a focus of financial and cultural interests, early on in the financial debacle, our Levitts are dealing with a world which, in their country at least, has set in motion forces which can only be inimical to the city. It is as difficult to compare one time to another as it is one place to another.

88. *To provide for the growth of cities we need to consider not how to simplify matters by mindless classification and separation of uses and activities, but how to complicate matters which are, and need to be, complex.* Paris suburb, Asnières.

True, however, that both phenomena have been produced out of the same basic socio-economic philosophy: the Adams in its juvenile stages, the Levitts in its decrepitude and decline. The basic philosophy was correct: to give to the people what the people wanted. One may ask, 'Is it still correct?' Should the more fortuned members of society still be given a choice which can only act in contradiction to what the whole of society needs, and wants? If every extension of the city in low-density high-cost patterns not only removes land from possible public use but also reduces the city in its financial potential, should those ex-urban land-grabs be permitted to continue? Levitt arid Sons did not invent the situation; they only exploited it. But having seen the result of their exploitation, are we prepared to continue on that track?

We are ensnared at present in a social, economic and cultural trap, which seems almost to preclude any impetus to reasonable urban development. We've trapped ourselves. By assuming that every extension of the city is simply an addition to it, we have taken an easy way out, a way which has become increasingly uneasy. None of us can maintain that the additions to our cities have demonstrated beyond refutation that suburbanization is the best way. The cities have acquired poisoned lands, as John Montague says, or waste land, as T. S. Eliot said, but they have acquired little else. As they extend their plastic suburbs into the country, their cores rot and grow old and cold. It is as if we had taken at the letter the advice of Alphonse Allais: 'If the city is so removed from nature as to become oppressive, there is a simple solution: move it to the country.' And, indeed we have seen many such outlandish proposals advanced by urbanists and administrators, such as Paris-Parallèle (by the *Architecture d'Aujourd'hui* group), the capital expansion plan for Washington 2000, etc. These are plans which propose that population increase in capital cities be accommodated in satellite developments, far outside the city, on cheap land. The satellites would be linked to the city by expressways and rail, in a kind of space and time machine concept. They are not properly extensions of the city, since they are remote, nor are they new cities since they are conceived only as bedroom accommodation for overflow from the existing city, on which they still depend for the major part of their economic, social and cultural base. They neglect to take into account the existing city, except as a rail or express way terminal. These plans all seem to say that the problem of metropolitan growth is so complex that our best answer is to ignore it entirely and to exploit new lands. There is an undeniable attraction in the idea of providing new bottles for the new wine. The attraction lies principally in its simplistic and schematic answer to an extremely complex problem. It is as if we were to say that when the game goes against us, or becomes difficult, we would change the rules of the game.

Unfortunately (or fortunately) this simple reasoning can only exist in its own intellectual void. We do not, in fact, have the power to change the rules of the game, for the 'game' is a monstrously complicated one involving all the citizens, and its rules have become the very essence of the political systems by which we live (which is not to say that they are entirely comprehensible to anybody). We may argue for a regional or national policy of urban growth, and we should, but such policy must of necessity account for an existing situation which is a complex of financial, political and even affective constraints. It must be a policy which works for us today, in our complicated urban–regional–national relationships, or else it is no policy but a pious wish.

The snare in which we find ourselves entangled is baited with 'progress,' technological and financial. As we advance along the path to 'higher standards of living,' without any clear idea of what 'living' is, we accumulate the tools which might destroy the city, and force us into isolation. The city cannot live with our new standards, e.g. the private automobile, the shopping center, the industrial 'park,' the office 'plaza.' All of these, products of each other, demand more space and looser communications than the urban environment can afford, and resources beyond our reach. In viewing the problem of urban growth and the extension of cities, we must attempt to seize appropriate tools to the job in hand. If our answer is 'more space' then we have only dodged the problem, not resolved it but ignored it. Cities have usually extended themselves in space-wasteful, low-density patterns, but never before have we had the occasion of doing something about it.

Today we are prisoners of chaotic urban growth only if we so choose. We have in most western countries evolved systems of law and finance which would permit our controlling urban growth. Those pieces of the systems which are yet missing can easily be supplied, and we can, and undoubtedly will, provide them in order to take effective control of our own environment. Then we will be really capable of raising our standard of living, as a society which may no longer be considered only as a mob of competing consumers. We already know, for instance, that no extension of the city is possible without adequate transportation, and we know that the privately owned motor car cannot provide that adequate transportation. We can show that the intensity of land use and the efficacy of transportation systems are indissolubly linked, just as space and time are. And these in turn are directly related to geographical distribution of various uses and functions. It is difficult but not impossible to coordinate the development of cities so as to accommodate smoothly all of these systems in a plan for growth, and to fashion the legal, financial and administrative tools to realize such a plan. After all, if such is our ambition, and we think that it clearly is, then we only need to make it plain to ourselves.

We have always thought of neighborhoods and boroughs and precincts as being in a sense towns within the city, each with its own character, and each being locally self-sufficient but linked to the others at a level of metropolitan need. We need only to apply the same ideas to our suburbs: to make them also self-sufficient towns within the city, rather than dormitory outposts lacking in services as well as in character. The character that they may take on is, of course, not a matter for legislative or administrative programming. It cannot be programmed-in, but it can be, and has been, programmed-out, excluded or inhibited through land-use planning practises which are either deliberately or inadvertently restrictive. Character comes with identity and how can such a non-viable organism as the low-density, single-use, single-class suburb acquire any identity? There is, as Gertrude Stein said, no there there. There is perhaps a dream of the bourgeoisie, the free-standing mini-villa or micro-chateau, at cut rates, but beyond that it is only a social, economic and ecological disaster area. As we see today in North America, not even the children of the suburbs, who know no other milieu, can identify with those suburbs. Similarly in France, England, Scandinavia and

89. *Dormitory outposts lacking in services as well as in character.* Drancy, outside Paris. It is of interest to note that the roads and parking places are asphalted while the footpaths are left unsurfaced.

90. *A social, economic and ecological disaster area ... the young are alienated within these isolated, incomplete and characterless residential zones.* Housing development in Nanterre, west of Paris. 'There is no there, there.'

Germany, the young are alienated within these isolated, incomplete and characterless residential zones.

It is difficult for us to judge whether it's best to extend existing cities, or to implant new ones. Whatever the approach, however, we can affirm that the urban spatial organization should be conceived as being as open and adaptable as possible. We are obliged to think in terms of rather massive interventions, as we try to catch up with the demand for new accommodation which has built up over years of neglect and ignorance of the true dimensions of the problems of urbanization. But even in dealing with the quantities with which we should be dealing, we can imagine dynamic, non-monumental, adaptable urban structures, which can be realized incrementally, modified in the course of realization and transformed over time to accommodate changes in programs and activities.

We have tried to develop such structures for new settlements, adapting a kind of basic linear structure (common to many villages) into a stem of activities which will support residential development at moderate densities. These stem projects indicate a way of thinking about new settlements which seems to us to be entirely consistent with the evolution of the new urban population. They are non-committal about urban form as being representative of social groupings; they seek to establish open-ended systems of development and to be adaptable to variations in density and intensity of use; they are intended to be non-centric in concept although it is assumed that they will become poly-centric through use. They also attempt to integrate various uses in a single system, by providing places for and services to, a variety of potential activities without, however, stratifying those uses prematurely. These proposals were presented in response to fairly precise development programs, with a view to demonstrating alternatives to the single-use zoned suburb.

Alternatives to exclusively residential development of the extensions of cities are constantly being sought, as in the Toulouse-le-Mirail scheme where an effort is made to associate some industrial, administrative and educational facilities which would provide at least a partial economic and institutional base for the new inhabitants as well as serving the region of Toulouse. Unfortunately the efforts here

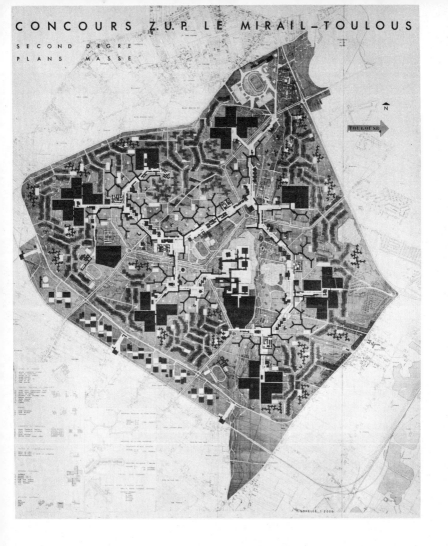

91. *In the Toulouse-le-Mirail scheme an effort is made to associate some industrial, administrative and educational facilities which would provide at least a partial economic and institutional base for the new inhabitants.* Plan of projected development at Toulouse-le-Mirail, a new settlement for 100,000 inhabitants. (Architects: Candilis, Josic and Woods.) It won first prize in a national urban design competition in 1961. High-rise housing along pedestrian spine with shops and social or cultural amenities. Schools grouped in educational parks at ends of pedestrian spine. In the center, a regional commercial and administrative center. Industry along south-western edge.

are somewhat undercut by a policy of segregated land use within the new development itself, so that it appears unlikely that any significant mix of uses in le-Mirail might ever be achieved. The difficulty arises from a misunderstanding of the question of scale in the new quarter. Distances are great and the bureaucratic tendency to lump uses into zones effectively precludes any real contact between the various activities. This is also a result of the low density imposed upon the new quarter, which makes in this case for high-rise residential buildings, surrounded and isolated by vast car-parks and unassigned space, industrial and educational parks surrounded by the same, and shopping 'malls,' and office 'plazas' placed far from the residential or industrial uses. The situation is aggravated by a total lack of transportation planning and policy: virtually all displacement within the site, and between the new and old quarters of Toulouse, must depend on the private motor car, to the joy of Renault and the despair of the inhabitants who thus are literally forced into the '*société bureaucratique à consommation dirigée*' as Henri Lefebvre describes it. One is obliged to conclude that le-Mirail, for all its image impact, cannot conceivably live up to the hopes which it generated at its inception (in a national urban design competition in 1961). It retains some architectural qualities which distinguish it from other, more desolate, housing projects in France, but will remain an urbanistic failure unless the rules can be changed, specifically the zoning rules which were imposed upon it, and which segregate rather than integrate the uses in what would otherwise be an admirable vocabulary.

It is clearly not enough simply to list desirable programs. Planning requires that space allocations be made, of course. The job of the urbanist is to put these together into a coherent whole with a sufficient uncertainty to allow for variations in both the nature of the programs and the disposition of the space. Toulouse-le-Mirail is, unfortunately, an example of the incoherence which land-use planning can produce. It represents a retreat from the principles of integration of uses and multi-functional distribution systems which it took as its bases. A magnificent opportunity to evolve those principles was lost, almost certainly through bureaucratic sloth and

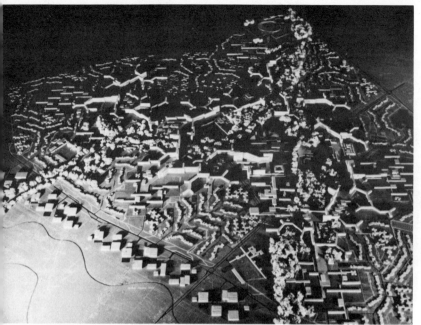

92. *It retains some architectural qualities which distinguish it from other, more desolate, housing projects.* Model of projected development at Toulouse-le-Mirail.

political timidity. It is never expedient to upset tradition, nor to implement new concepts in urbanism and urban land use, until it becomes impossible to do otherwise.

Although Toulouse-le-Mirail seems doomed to underachievement, having been insufficiently supported at the administrative level of implementation (and perhaps insufficiently understood at the urban design level of conception) there is no good reason for abandoning the principles which were there poorly translated into design. The schemes from which le-Mirail was distilled, Caen-Hérouville and Bilbao—Val d'Asua, may still be mined for ideas. The principle of 'Stem' development which is embodied in them remains valid and their essential comprehensibility may yet illuminate other planning

93. *Caen-Hérouville still may be mined for ideas.* Model of proposed development at Caen-Hérouville for 40,000 inhabitants. (Architects: Candilis, Josic, Woods.) Organization of high- and low-rise dwellings along a pedestrian stem of commercial, educational, social and cultural facilities. At this time (1961) it was felt that the stem would directly serve relatively dense development in high buildings (six, ten, fourteen stories). Stacked modular walk-ups and terrace housing was arranged in low-density infill patterns or clusters further out from the stem. (cf. Bilbao.) The longest dimension of the stem (top to bottom, or left to right on the plate) is about twenty minutes walk.

The form of the high-rise buildings indicated here does not derive from any architectural consideration other than the following: 1) since part of the pedestrian circulation system is contained within these buildings, connecting access points, at the stem or at car parks, to the dwellings, the plan is designed to accommodate easy movement with gradual rather than abrupt change in direction. 2) The open angle reduces overlooking and overshadowing from one part of the building to another. 3) Limiting the number of access points allows a larger measure of control over the amount of land which can be taken for the private vehicle, leaving more safe, open landscaped space for the people.

problems in other regions, in spite of (or perhaps because of) their having been ultimately rejected *in toto* by local, regional and national planning and development administrations.

The Stem idea is not new. It seeks to re-establish old and tried principles of association of human activities in contemporary situations.

We do not necessarily need to re-invent 'new' forms, even though we are dealing with a new man in a new world. He is still a man, moving at man-speed when he can, and associating with other men for most of his human needs. The new world in which he lives is a continuation and a rebirth of the old world in which his ancestors lived. The law of gravity, like other physical laws, may be hard but it is still the law: *Dura lex, sed lex.* There are, to be sure, new constraints and new opportunities, chiefly technological. There is a new sense of limit and number, visibly and palpably. We would maintain that, in the growth and extension of cities, these new parameters are certainly influential but they do not *a priori* exclude old geometries or known forms of urban association.

In all of the speculation about urban life and form to which we have been subject in the past decade, none appears to us so desolate as the desperate with-it-ness of the young architects and urbanists who are inspired by super-graphics, computer-graphics, and the paraphernalia of moonshots and war machines. In their well-meaning indignation with a stagnant state of affairs they have gone far beyond the realm of reasonable reaction and thus have found themselves isolated in a science-fiction (pseudo-science) world of their own creating. Normally this might attract no particular comment but administrators have become so harassed as the years of failure begin to weigh upon them, that these software jokes are seen as a kind of life-saver, which will at least take people's minds off their present problems, and take some pressure off the administration. So we have an institutionalized science-fiction, gingerly backed by the powers that rule our cities, as a diversion. The architects of this enterprise are truly the servants of an oppressive regime, lending their undeniable talents to the furtherance of an unsupportable *status quo* by proposing inconceivable alternatives. The outrageous character of

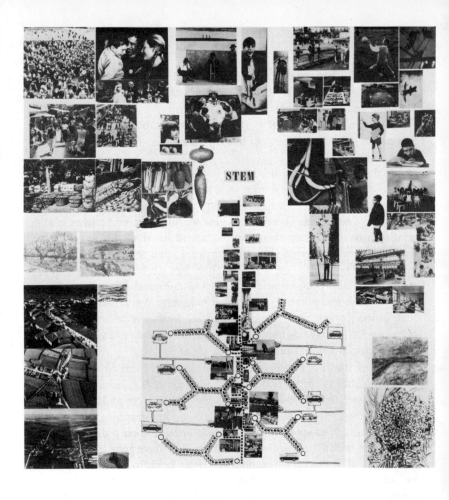

their proposals serves only to reinforce the sweet reasonableness of repression.

The Stem idea is an attempt, not to reject new forms and return to old ones, but to choose among possible forms that one which best adapts to modern exigencies. The necessity for such a choice resides in the pitiful inadequacy of any modern alternative. There is no modern, i.e. different and new, form of urban association. There are only schematics for dissociation and dispersal. The challenge of finding an urban form suitable and adequate for twentieth-century man has not been met but eluded by discarding any comprehensible form of association. That is why it was felt necessary to re-examine the choices available in the second half of this century, and the stem proposal for urban extension was made.

The first Stem proposal was printed in May 1960, in *Architectural Design* (no. 5, p. 181), and was used as the basis for the plans submitted for Caen-Hérouville and Bilbao—Val d'Asua in 1961. In

94. *The Stem idea* ... Montage of the Stem idea, which reveals the preoccupation with people and their daily activities that lies behind this attempt to rationalize the urban design process by reintroducing as: 1) the comprehensible ordering of urban space for commercial and individual activities, and 2) the acceptance of change in both function and form of these activities over long and short cycles of time, as the generators of plans for large-scale developments. The second of these imperatives obviously conditions the first, so that the ordering of activities takes place, as far as possible, in a non-formal organization. Thus Stem is linear: a line has no dimension and can change direction at will. It is assumed that the dwellings will tend to change on a long-term cycle while their ancillaries, the social, educational, cultural and commercial facilities will adapt to a short cycle of change. The ancillaries are grouped in a linear fashion (the Stem) which serve the dwelling groups that plug into the stem. Density can be varied, adjusting to the intensity of use along the stem.

This is essentially a pedestrian system of circulation. A mass transit system can be superimposed to connect various points, as in the Bilbao scheme (see illustration nos. 96–8, pp. 176, 178), but it would probably not follow the same path; it operates peripherally and has access to the Stem only at points. Motor and pedestrian scales are irreconcilable, hence they are segregated.

essence the proposal attacked the then current practice of massing volumes, generated by combinations of dwellings, in more or less subtle arrangements dictated by architectural design considerations. 'Stem' proposed to rationalize the design process by introducing (or rather reintroducing) other imperatives such as the comprehensible ordering of the real (as opposed to the geometric) disposition of community activities, and the acceptance of change in function and form of these activities, as fundamental generators of plans for large-scale developments. This recognition of the determinants of our environment was, and remains, essential. The geometries of architectural composition, however fetching, are clearly inadequate to the problems of urban growth, as indeed they always were (e.g. *Palma Nuova, les Salines de Chaux* and other time-stopping schemes of previous centuries). We can safely put behind us any such notions, having tried them again and found them inadequate again in our time. The urbanists who could conceive of such well-tempered schemes were dealing with other preoccupations than ours. Even in the eighteenth and nineteenth centuries it was still conceivable that a definitive urban form might be found, and that that form might correspond to basic human needs and desires. In our century, it is seen that no such form could exist, since we have other, and evolving, needs and desires. The shape of society is blurred, and the shape of society's cities cannot be established on any basis of formal composition. Our aspirations are toward non-formal, or informal, arrangements, in any case. Any attempt to reverse that trend seems doomed from the beginning. We are left then with a kind of design vacuum, since we proclaim that design in itself is not good enough. What, one wonders, will be good enough to order the mass of buildings which must be produced and installed in the space around existing cities?

We suggest then that cities can be extended, but that their extension must follow some kind of order, in order to avoid chaos. Order must be comprehensible; patterns of growth must include a pattern understandable by the citizens. Stem provides a method of ordering growth, of organizing it in a non-formal, dynamic way, adaptable to change, and completely comprehensible to the citizens. It is not

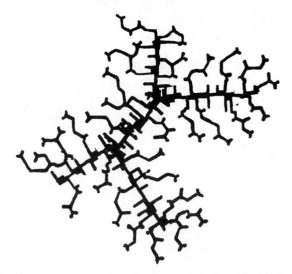

95. *Order must be comprehensible, patterns of growth must include a pattern comprehensible to the citizens. Stem provides a method of ordering growth, of organizing it in a non-formal, or informal, dynamic way, adaptable to change and completely comprehensible to the citizens.* Abstract of proposed plan for Caen-Hérouville, showing built pedestrian circulation system extending from stem into dwelling complex, connecting access points. (The stem itself is not built; it is open urban space, defined by buildings, at the natural ground level, paved and planted appropriately.)

nearly enough to locate the required building masses, in the same way that one fills in a crossword puzzle, following the program for each function separately. One must relate the functions to each other and to the entire complex of human habitat, and this is what we have attempted to illustrate in these proposals. They are fairly simple and should, in a reasonable context, even appear as commonplace.

Unfortunately we do not always work within a reasonable context. It is necessary to reaffirm the importance of interrelating functions because so much emphasis has been placed recently on functionalism, i.e. on an ideal location and form for each function. Functionalism in architecture and urbanism has turned out to be somewhat like providing exhaustive dictionaries of definitions of words with no

VALLEE

96. Model of proposed development at Val d'Asua, near Bilbao. Pedestrian-oriented stems of activity are distributed along the crests, automobile access uses the valleys. Topography determines the overall geometry in the disposition of the stem.

In contrast to the plan proposed for Caen-Hérouville, the low-rise development has been placed along the stem. In both schemes the spine of pedestrian circulation, the stem, is at the natural ground level and is paved as needed (contrast with Toulouse-le-Mirail where the stem is a continuous platform over parking, an intimidating and expensive solution).

97. Plan showing distribution of social, cultural, educational and commercial facilities for a development in the Val d'Asua area outside Bilbao. These are arranged to form a stem of activities, pedestrian-oriented, which supports and serves 20,000 dwellings. Light industrial development is proposed along the peripheral roads at the ends of the stem.

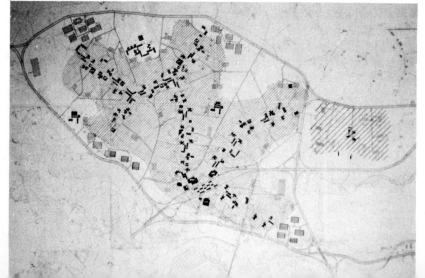

preoccupation for syntax or grammar, or how words combine to function veritably as part of a communications system. We do not reject architectural or urbanistic functionalism, but we would say that the dictionary is not enough when we are called upon to speak of problems of human settlement. The functions, no matter how well we define each, finally must be tied together in a functioning urban system.

In the thirties, the CIAM* were able to distil out of urban life four principal functions: living, working, circulation and recreation. These categories were useful in their time and produced startling results when cities were analyzed in relation to them. By the fifties, it was seen that analysis, however penetrating, was not a sufficient basis for planning, and that the four functions were important to understanding the workings of the city, but inadequate alone as disciplines for design. It became obvious that the relationships between those functions define also the relationships of the citizen to his urban world.

We feel strongly that these relationships are largely indefinable. They cannot be fixed in any permanent pattern; they will tend continually to shift, even for individuals. For communities they are constantly changing. In the proposals which grew out of the stem idea, we try to indicate how those shifting relationships can best be accommodated, by defining long- and short-term cycles of change (in itself a functionalist approach) and organizing the public domain to remain responsive to short-term change cycles while the private domain reacted to the long-term change cycle. By doing this, we felt that the entire urban complex could more readily be adapted to the changing needs and desires of the citizens; their dwellings however would remain stable over the life of the family, at least. This line of reasoning seems to us still relevant today, and especially for new extensions to the city. Despite disavowals from the left, the family nucleus of society flourishes and demands adequate accommodation, in ownership if possible. We cannot see how this demand can justifiably be denied when it can easily be satisfied, it being understood that ownership does not necessarily mean acquisition and control of

* See note, Chap. 1, p. 70.

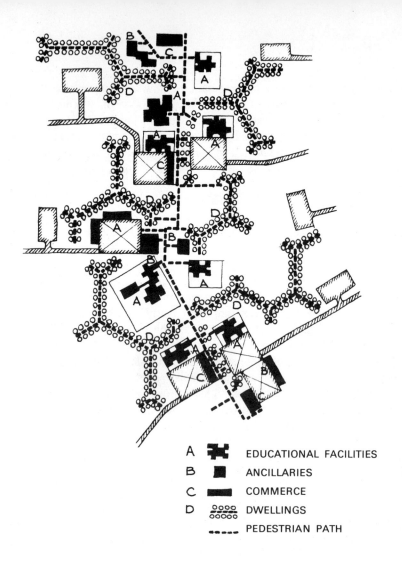

A	EDUCATIONAL FACILITIES	
B	ANCILLARIES	
C	COMMERCE	
D	DWELLINGS	
	PEDESTRIAN PATH	

98. Diagram of Stem idea as applied in Bilbao–Val d'Asua proposals. The diagram for Caen-Hérouville is similar, except that in Bilbao it was decided to bring the low-rise, walk-up buildings into direct contact with the stem, rather than relegating them to the periphery. Thus the pedestrian circulation system connects to all dwellings. Automobile access is still controlled and limited to points from which easy and comfortable access to dwellings may be obtained.

99. Diagrammatic cross-section through stem, showing how dwellings are linked through a continuous collective pedestrian circulation system to the stem, with lower buildings (walk-ups) developing along the stem. Pedestrian circulation is indicated in broken lines, ancillaries in black. Garaging and servicing is accommodated below grade at intervals, with plazas, play spaces and light construction above. The covered parking space near the stem, like the open car parks at the edges of the development are located to provide limited but easy access to vertical circulation cores serving the dwellings.

This section reveals how the stem and the buildings which it serves would be related to the topography. The crest of the hill belongs to the public. The highest points are open, urban space. What we used to do for the gods, then for the kings, we now can do for the people.

100. *All urban arrangements might be reduced to either stems or webs ... The terminology is insignificant ... The only important thing is that both these terms translate into comprehensible, human-scaled, coherent urban worlds.* A representation of stem: Stemsville, human-scaled and free of the space-consuming, visually-offensive, noisome motor car. There could be a there, there.

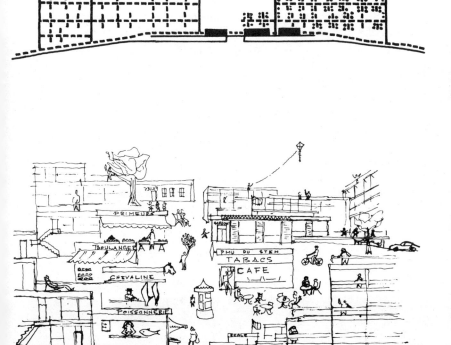

a plot of ground but simply of a dwelling. On the other hand, it seems ever more essential to keep open the options on the location and character of the ancillaries which serve those dwellings immediately and the other functions to which they relate, on the metropolitan scale, such as places of work and means of transport.

The Stem idea includes all these possibilities. In a fairly loose but comprehensible association of activities it can serve as a support to a variety of dwelling types. By its nature it is open, i.e. adaptable. Carefully planned, it can restore the street to the pedestrian while allowing motor vehicles to render the real services which their mobility makes possible. It can accommodate other forms of transportation as long as their characteristics are not incompatible with the idea of the street. Since it is basically a pedestrian-orientated system it can presumably offer an enduring and inexpensive answer to the questions of how to organize new settlements in the light of evolving speculative transportation techniques. In any mass transit system we know that eventually the initial and final connections will be made on foot, just as we know that the ultimate justification of mass transit is its efficiency in terms of space, time and investment.

All urban arrangements, in terms of building, infrastructure and equipment, can be reduced to either stems or webs. We have suggested, in Chapter 2 of this book, that webs of activities are natural to the inner city. Here we suggest that stems are natural in the development of new extensions to the city, since as the city grows undeveloped land must be conserved. It is probable that both stems and webs will be combined in any large-scale development, each configuration having its own scale. A web is a network of stems, a stem is ultimately part of a web and may serve many smaller webs. The terminology is insignificant, however useful it may be to urbanists. The only important thing is that both these terms translate into comprehensible, human-scaled, coherent urban worlds.

4. The Planning of Regions Around and Between Cities

Although we often may think that we have passed beyond the traditional interdependence of cities and their regions, the thought is indeed transitory. Cities still depend upon their immediate hinterlands; rural activities are still dependent upon urban markets, and they often exist in much closer relationships than we generally understand. To think of city and country inevitably conjures up images of trade, industry and agriculture, all of which are outmoded, turn-of-the-century words. However, and however unstylish it may be, these words still serve best to describe what it is that city- and country-folk do that makes them part of a continuing symbiosis of trade and industry on the one hand, agriculture and mining on the other. These are obviously activities which can scarcely be carried on simultaneously in the same place. Yet any development in one of them must affect the others; changes in the rural sector produce immediate change in the cities, and vice versa. As agriculture (or mining) evolves from a labor-intensive to a mechanized capital-intensive enterprise, cities are affected by an enrichment of the labor market in much the same unwilling way that streams and rivers are enriched beyond endurance by phosphate run-off from agricultural fertilizers. Conversely, when trade and industry could no longer use an over-enriched labor supply, agriculture and mining have endured brief periods of low wages and inadequately applied standards of safety and security. The labor force is shuffled between these poles. In the first half of this century, in most western countries, we have seen an exodus from the land and from the mines, largely caused by the introduction of new machinery and new economic theory. The latter seeks to demonstrate that labor is dispensable when the task can be performed as well, or nearly as well, by machines, however

101. *As agriculture evolves from a labor-intensive to a mechanized, capital-intensive entreprise* . . . Harvest in North Dakota.

102. *This form of capital-intensive farming and mining has driven many productive persons from rural areas toward the city, that 'El Dorado' with its beckoning promises.* Shantytown in Paris suburb of Nanterre. Photograph taken from the window of a new student residence. Repression and revolt are in the air.

expensive they may be. This form of capital-intensive farming and mining has driven many productive persons from rural areas toward the city, that 'El Dorado' with its beckoning promises. In fact, the only place where dislocated miners and dispossessed farmers could hope to find a fair deal, or any deal, was in the urban chaos. It is unfortunate that no thought was given to this problem when bureaucratic technocrats and agribusiness entrepreneurs were 'streamlining' the primary enterprises of these countries. Hordes of figures are produced to show that the change is for the better, but none take into account the human problems created by an enormous labor surplus. So we have whipped out from under them the means of support of a

significant number of people, like tablecloth magic, with no program for their continued existence. Free market capitalism is supposed to take care of that, and the resultant misery and poverty is seen as an unfortunate but necessary incident in our unstoppable march to . . . what? What compelling chimera could guide us through such inhuman policies?

Nonetheless, the problem has been created. Vast numbers of people have been evicted from their former livings (which perhaps were none too good) and dumped into the urban environment. Some of them come to expand the numbers employed in industry, others to fill service jobs, and many are thrown to the mercy of relief and welfare. Homes must be provided as well as jobs. And so the city grows, randomly, while the country, corporatized, grows barren of human habitat.

The industrialization of the countryside leads directly to the deterioration of the city. There is presumed to be a national administration which watches over all this, but it seems to be dead, or at least out of order. As the locus of 'economic' problems shifts around the country, obeying laws which are perhaps simple but secret, the administration flails about, attacking imaginary, however imaginable, problems. Not often do we come back to the complex problems of cities, or cities in their region, or the national policy on cities. Yet millions of dollars and decades of time are spent on the primary production problem – agriculture and mines – without ever a thought to the cities which lie beyond the deserted mines and bankrupt farms. It is as though the bad capitalists wished to live up to their worst press, as tyrants and exploiters of the common man. Rarely has the world seen such a debacle, on a grand scale, as the dislocation from a rural to an urban economy in the western countries. This colossal social failure will live with us for many generations, each of which will perhaps find, as we have found, some absurdly clever way of dissociating itself from responsibility for its continuance ('you can't stop progress') and thereby creating or increasing its own alienation from its own psychological milieu, in a world which it knows to be ever more closely knit. The tendency appears to be suicidal.

103. *Nevertheless the problem has been created. Vast numbers of people have been evicted from their former livings (which were perhaps none too good)* ... Farm in southern United States.

104. *The cities which lie beyond the deserted mines and bankrupt farms.* Children of Appalachian emigrants in Chicago. Strip mining, a particularly vicious form of despoliation, has removed their land from them.

We are devoted to a cult of progress, but unable to conceive of, or be bothered with an equal progress in a social sense. The progress which we achieve in organizing agriculture and mining has no counterpart in urban development. Our vision seems always to be limited, perversely, to a single segment of the economy, or to a privileged category of society. The theory seems to be that benefits in a 'higher economic' sector (i.e. a sector which produces greater returns on money invested) will automatically engender benefits in all sectors. This is the theory of 'spin-off,' according to which great concentration of wealth or knowledge will presumably throw off large gobs of beneficial material, indiscriminately, to the masses. It is undoubtedly a comfortable theory, in whose name almost any excess may be justified, from rural land-grabs to moonshots. It does not however seem to have any verifiable basis in tangible fact. The moon decade in America has been accompanied by an accelerating impoverishment of the economically weak. The consolidation and industrialization of large agrarian holdings, the *latifundia* of North America, has swollen the numbers of unemployed and welfare recipients in the cities. 'Spin-off' may exist, but its beneficial effects to the society at large are clearly insignificant, indeed undetectable. We have nothing to show for all our progress and we must therefore conclude that this progress is reserved to a certain class, a fragment of society which, in a dispassionate description, would be called parasitic. We can see then that the tendency is not suicidal but more simply colonial. It is, however, nonetheless irrational when viewed from a sufficiently detached position. Money and means are increasingly concentrated; greater and more pressing disparities are created. We cannot say that this is progress, in a social or human sense. It looks more like panic, with the wealthy defending their wealth in an infernally nonsensical cycle. What do they do with their wealth? Some transform it into power, by operating tax-exempt foundations which perform para-governmental services of research and development, always with an eye to controlling the use of their money for the ultimate benefit of themselves. Others build 'empires' of speculation, multi-national corporations to defraud the Internal Revenue Service and further their personal security by overseas diversification. Most, we suspect, merely count their wealth and measure themselves against each other in some obscene dynastic competition for status.

It is clear that any reasonable regional or national policy of development will need to overcome this short-sightedness of the capitalist system. In the same way that we can say that the rights of private enterprise do not include the right to pollute the public's air and water, we can say that the rights of free enterprise do not include the right to manipulate social ecology. Any regional or national policy would need to impose a new set of rules, which would rule out the most blatant abuses of the free market economic system, i.e. those which create and maintain a structural impoverishment of a part of the people. Clearly the relative enrichment of even the greater number cannot be used any longer as a justification for dislocating and degrading even one person, let alone the millions, the hundreds of millions, who are sacrificed to the concept of progress. If the robber barons can still make money under the new rules then they may perhaps be allowed their vicious pleasures. It seems, however, extremely unlikely that they could continue, since money-making and social responsibility appear to be mutually exclusive. If this is the case then we must, with no regrets, leave them to other devices and get on with the business of making a better world for every person on earth.

The city and its region are still interdependent and, indeed, are so intimately linked that we might, rather than consider a country as being occasionally punctuated by cities, imagine that a country or continent is really one big city with very large, under-populated holes in it. The entire continental complex in Europe or America tends more and more to function as a whole, a web of interdependent parts. Boroughs, cities, counties, regions are no longer really operating as independent entities. As in the domino theory, each is shoring up the other.

It may be to our advantage to reconsider our countries in this way: the city of England, the city of Europe, the city of North America. Since it has become obvious that fragmented administration of isolated municipalities can only lead to stupid competition for national support (no city in the present form can survive on its own); should we not assemble the whole national or even continental mess into one? The proliferation of administrative entities, each presuming to operate from its own tax base, (and none succeeding) has led only to a grievous imbalance in the distribution of wealth, which is, after all, a national resource and should be available to all on an equitable basis. Any proposal for national cities may sound at first like a super-concentration of power into the hands of a single administration but I believe that the fears which it arouses may be allayed somewhat by a consideration of the ways in which municipal, as opposed to state, politics now work. The day by day improvisation which characterizes most municipal administrations dealing with local, community-controlled power structures should be exemplary to regional or national governments. The proposal is not to concentrate power into the hands of a single administration but to diffuse power in municipal type political structures while associating it with direct responsibility to community-controlled lobbies. It is to be hoped that by running our countries as cities we might reduce existing regional inequities and bring administrative chicanery under control. We should reconsider and probably reject the old, inherited administrative structures, in the light of our realization that there is now total interdependence of urban, suburban, exurban and rural settlements. Systems of government which evolved for small-scaled, widespread patterns of settlement, loosely linked, are no longer adequate, now that the land is fully occupied and means of communication are increasingly efficient. Nations and continents are ever more closely tied together in a web of instantaneous communication and ultra-rapid transportation.

Distance is no longer meaningful. Measured by time, it becomes a variable. In electronic telecommunications it disappears altogether as the world enjoys a banquet in Peking or a football match in Brazil. Only at the human, pedestrian scale of speed does distance retain the significance it once had. We must then seek ways of changing the old administrative hodge-podge of local, regional and national political system, which accounts neither for the old pedestrian micro-scale (since it has, perforce, been influenced by these changes) nor for the new technological macro-scale (since it has not been able to respond adequately to them). We would be well advised, in an urbanizing world, to look to the most highly evolved systems, i.e. our municipal governments, for models of administration and government which can be adapted to both these scales, since they both exist, and will continue for any forseeable time. I'd suggest that the most responsive, least oppressive, most evolutive systems of government that most countries have achieved are their municipal systems, which must remain reactive to immediate public needs, or perish. The suggestion that nations, and eventually continents, be municipalized, is made in this sense, of installing responsive government. One would hope, through this device, to promote the most vital elements of our present systems – undoubtedly the city form of government – at the expense of parliaments, houses of congress, senates, cabinets of ministers, super-cabinets, presidents *e tutti quanti*.

If we propose intensified community control, which naturally adjusts to the enduring human scale, we should also construct administrative systems which are appropriate to the new and changing super-scale of intensified communication and expanding urbanization. However I do not think that these necessary new systems are best imagined in hierarchical schemes of ever-larger dominating elements such as we now know, going from hamlet to nation, in a structure where responsibility and power are dissociated. For whatever reasons, people in cities seem to have kept a closer rapport with their chosen representatives and hence a closer control over them than that reflected in national assemblies. My suggestion, then, is that we should attempt to transpose the municipal form of government, which has less heirarchical structure and a more intimate association of power and responsibility, to the national, continental and global scale.

The national, continental (eventually global) city would be such a super-scaled administrative structure, much closer to our present urban and rural realities than the creaking, feudal systems under which we now labor. Just as there is no fixed functional social unit larger than the household and smaller than the city, so we would say that there is no workable administrative unit larger than the community and smaller than the country. The seeming contradiction here

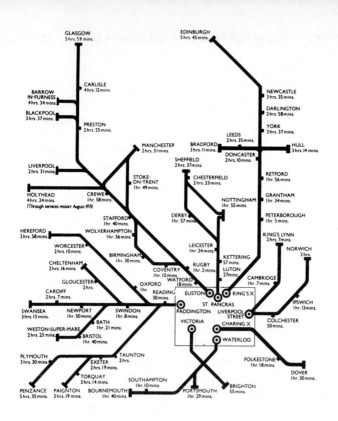

105. *In the light of our realization that there is now total interdependence of urban, suburban, exurban and rural settlements.* (top left) British Rail map showing relative time-distances and links to the London underground.

106. *Only at the human, pedestrian scale of speed does distance retain the significance it once had.* (left) Hobo, walking the track in California.

107. *A hierarchical scheme of ever-larger dominating units . . . building up to a central government, a system in which responsibility and power are dissociated and diffused in archaic patterns.* (above) State opening of Parliament in London.

comes from the fact that we are talking about two different kinds of
association. The community is a comprehensible unit which is larger
than the household and smaller than the city. However, it is not an
administrative unit since it varies in size and boundaries according to
its preoccupations. It is elusive, indefinable. The school community is
not the same for various levels of schooling. One household may be
part of more than one community and, conversely, a community may
embrace varying numbers of households, depending upon its
vocation and/or its evolution over a time. Communities are what
they decide they will be; large or small they create themselves as they
perceive their identities. They change themselves as their problems
and preoccupations change. They are not, then, concrete administrative entities, but real groups of people with common concerns.
They are real, and they are therefore ephemeral. They exist but
cannot be defined in numerical, or often in geographical, administrative terms. They are not subject to stratification. They are interest
groups, and they must, and will, be taken into account, but they vary
constantly.

Concrete administrative entities such as wards, districts, counties,
etc., are necessarily abstract since they have always been, and perhaps can only be, determined by numbers, size or area, in political
terms. This administrative composition cannot respond to the actual
population which determines it, i.e. the people themselves, in their
various communities of race, sex, age, philosophies, styles and preoccupations. It is in the intention of reducing this abstract, administrative absurdity that we would propose a single administration
which we would call a city, since that seems to us to be the most
fitting term. City describes the intent and purpose of society without
any of the spurious emotional overtones which overload such words
as nation, fatherland, *patria*. It also carries the connotation of a
functioning physical entity. We know what a city is, and has been,
and we can project our image of a city into a continental organization
quite readily, once we shift the scale. City and community are ideas
with which we can work. They are also realities, which we can easily
recognize: the vast, responsive city administration on the one hand,
the intense community concern on the other. Each completes the

other; there is no need and no place for intermediate administrative systems between the community in its varying constellations and the city with its overall responsibilities. Since it is clearly true that what happens in Washington happens to New York, and what happens in Paris happens to Lille; we are suggesting only that the effect be moved closer to its cause, that Washington be made more responsive to New York (or Paris to Lille) by becoming part of it; that taxes be collected and money distributed without recourse to such costly administrative fictions as the sub-division of countries into states, of states into counties and towns, of towns into boroughs and wards; that the multitude of bureaucracies which are necessary to administer the continent (of Europe, of North America) be welded into one, and the repressive inconsistencies removed.

The new city, continental in size, as the administrative unit, could not fail to be more responsive, as well as more efficient, than the present hierarchies of geopolitical precedence, authority and responsibility. It would be more responsive because it would react, not to arbitrary geographical or numerical constituencies, but to real common-interest communities, not on a basis of average representation (as the national systems now work) but on a basis of real representation of interests held in common by communities of people. There might at a given time, for instance, be several representatives from one geographical area, each speaking for a different community within that area. Or there might be only one, who could speak for all. Or there might be one who could speak for several areas. Representation in the City Council then should be conceived to reflect the real interests of the people represented. Differences and similarities in interests would probably tend to be more accentuated. At least we could clearly understand and appreciate the parliamentary process. The New City Council would represent all the forces (communities) of the city. Americans may object that this would upset their vaunted system of 'checks and balances,' just as the French or Italians may find it too simple for their political traditions. But think what possibilities might spring from the continental city.

In the beginning, at least there could be a renewal of faith in egalitarian social democracy. One man would equal one vote, at the

New City-wide level. Government (since we must have it) would, or could, be directly accessible to the people. It would be operating as a function of their immediate concerns: food, shelter, health, learning, as well as philosophy, technology and planetary responsibility. Economic and physical planning could be attempted and, more importantly, could be revised or rejected when shown to be deficient. War and defense, essentially artificial issues, could be brought back to their proper level, as the very least of our concerns. (Who ever heard, recently, of a war between cities? Or of a city with a 'defense' budget, wasting one third to one half of its resources?)

Since it is our primary concern in this book, we are mostly interested in the economic and physical planning potential of the New City. It is ironic that one of the newest suburban excrescences of New York, in Rockland County, is called New City. The city of New City does not exist; it is represented by a sign on a highway, which says New City. There is nothing there. But if we think of what New City might be, did it not encompass a few square miles of Rockland County, but all the square miles of all the counties of North America, we may be flabbergasted (to use an old Yankee expression). The veritable New City, which encompasses a continent, would naturally release all sorts of surprises. The mayor of Chicago, or the *maire* of Dijon, would find themselves in a position of political impotence, since they could only represent their immediate communities with any validity. But their communities, having been integrated into a much larger administrative scheme, would be forced to discover anew the levers of political power, and to recognize that eventually all power remains to the people, and that popular interests could very well ignore ancient administrative boundaries.

Chicago and Dijon (or Halifax and Liverpool) would not cease to exist. Their identities could only be reinforced by integrating them, as special places, in the New City. No one will argue for the elimination, or even the blurring, of the identity of those places; one will only argue that they should take their place in a total environmental scheme. We cannot, unfortunately, imagine any governmental organization, in which those special places (all places are special) might be accommodated so well as in the New Continental City.

The problem of identity becomes a real one when such schemes as the continental or global city are put forth. However, we should consider two factors: what is the content of identity and to whom are we addressing ourselves? What are we talking about, and to whom? We cannot but feel that, whatever the disadvantages, citizens create a certain rapport or relationship to their cities. The rapport is often frivolous, based upon jokingly negative aspects such as 'The Windy City' (for Chicago), but in every case they generate a sense of place and belonging, i.e. of identity of the citizen and his city. The citizens know where they are. If the city limits are abandoned, and Chicago, Lille and Liverpool become administratively parts of the great cities of America, France or England, need this feeling of identity be lost? We do not feel that it will be, or could be. The issue is a false one. The real content of identity cannot be removed, from cities any more than from races. The Milanese, a different race from the Roman, has created, and will sustain, a different urban milieu. In the city of Italy, the identity of the component parts will probably endure. We do not see this as an obstacle to the administrative reorganization of the Italian subcontinent. On the contrary, the maintaining of local identities can only enrich the concept of non-hierarchical administration. We will all, Milanesi, and Romani, be citizens of the great city of Italy, or Europe, but will not squander our identity on indeterminate, intermediate, artificial regional structures of government.

There are however enormous difficulties in our proposal. We would urge a complete reorganization of government and administration but in order to achieve it we need to dislodge a complex of bureaucracies and men who have considerable interest in keeping the *status quo*. We wish to eliminate a hierarchical system of privilege and authority which is literally killing us, but how to persuade the men to whose immediate personal advantage the system seems to work, to join us in reforming the system? Among the bureaucrats there are many who are uneasy with the workings of the system, and who would welcome a change. Among those who choose to enter the system there are many, perhaps most, who are well-motivated and to whom we may speak in convincing and credible terms, which we can do if we are ourselves convinced of the appropriateness and adequacy of the proposals. It is not reasonable to expect cooperation in countering the interests of those who hold power if all we can offer in exchange for their relinquishing it is such an ephemeral reward as a good conscience. There will undoubtedly be a growing fifth column within the bureaucracy and some reformers among the elected officials, but the mass of the power structure can be relied upon to guard jealously its present status and areas of power, if not to extend them.

The big question then is whether or not we can hope for reform in the bureaucratic societies of the west or whether the only conceivable change is to be a violent redistribution of power. In this context the Continental City may at first appear to be more of an attitude, a way of thinking about political and physical environments than a feasible scheme for their reorganization. However there is a direct relationship between attitude and action. When we say that cities of the world should unite, we are attempting to project an attitude into an action. We are recognizing that human habitat is a totally integrated and interdependent system, organized around urban settlements essentially, and that any other basis of organization can only be colonial (e.g. the US today, where the so-called 'silent majority' is major by its power, not by its numbers). The Continental City is a concept on which to base action aimed at redressing such colonial situations, recognizing and stimulating the inherent power of numbers. It states that urbanism is economy, ecology and government. These can be dissociated, as they are at present, but the risks of social strife, economic inequity and ecological disaster have grown to intolerable levels during this dissociation. A change is therefore inevitable, and the necessary change back to a reintegration of the social, economic and physical environments could well be directed along the lines of the Continental City.

We're heavily invested by exurban powers and persons, notably the War Departments, which have no urban links. The military–industrial establishment in most countries is completely non-urban, except in its source of funds, which is mostly urban. This is an outrageous exploitation of the city dwellers by non-city forces. Can these forces be contained? Or is revolution, the violent redressing of wrongs, inevitable? Certainly it may prove to be unavoidable under present conditions and projected trends.

Continental City is seen as a way to begin to correct the iniquities of non-urban domination over the urban majority. Can evolution of political thinking ever displace revolution as an approach toward the bettering of human habitat? It ought to be possible to correct the course, before the ship founders on the reef of exploitation and oppression. Whether in western Europe, North America or the Antipodes, means must be found to forestall a bloody confrontation, which daily becomes more possible, between the affluent and powerful and the deprived. Why do we think the confrontation may be bloody? Why indeed need there be any confrontation? To those who wish, or think, that all's well, we would suggest an investigation in depth of the unbelievably inhuman conditions which exist in and around our 'great' cities. The slums and shanty towns, which are the only habitat accessible to rural persons displaced by the great God-machine of industrial progress in agriculture, are not filled only with quiescent victims. Men are being degraded and some of them will surely fight back. There is no concept of progress, in the sense in which bureaucrats use the term, which might be understandable to those men, women and children, who only see continuing misery in their overcrowded slums. Continental City might be a way, to establish (or in some cases re-establish) a working democracy – a government and an economy which would be for the people. And for what else should the government and the economy be?

Our concern, as urbanists, is to conceive of systems which destroy The System. The System is clearly based upon the oppression of some people, often the majority, by others. It is a System worthy of destruction, a dragon which must be slain if we are to progress beyond the Slough of Despond in our pursuit of a better life for every person on earth. We know that the exploiters, the bureaucrats and capitalists, are already and always in pursuit of a better life, but seemingly only for themselves. It is not clear in what way their life could be better, even to them. However, power continues to corrupt, infinitely and absolutely, and the men in positions of power continue to be hopelessly corrupted, to the point where they lose contact with the realities of everyday human existence. Locked up in their ridiculous perquisites (exemplified by the executive toilet) they lose even the sense of their own humanity. We need to break down the doors and barriers which they have erected between themselves and life. Continental City may be a key to open the doors, or eventually a battering-ram to knock them down. In any case, it is a tool which we can conceive to refashion those attitudes which have resulted in misery for the greater number and alienation for everybody. To govern with the people, and for them, one doesn't need to have the key to an executive toilet, but a key to those executive attitudes which can be productive. We see, at present, only executive bankruptcy, plastered over with status symbols, as though (as in the executive toilet) the image were more important than the function. The impulse to execute the executives is growing ever stronger, while their prerogatives grow ever more silly and, as a consequence, respect for their function declines. How can one treat seriously a functionary whose only ambition is to amass more and more power (money or status) with which he can finally only open toilet doors, or restaurant doors? We grant that their jobs (corporation presidents or chairmen, prime ministers, etc.) are thankless, and we often wonder what sort of fool would aspire to such positions, but after all, they themselves create and perpetuate those thankless positions, and through their witless greed for power, assure that the positions will be thankless. We see these men – they are only men – perform ludicrously in public, daily; we cannot be expected to respect either the men or the high offices which they are supposed to fill. Since they cannot, by the nature of The System, fill those high positions adequately, they must perforce bring the positions low, down to their own level. This is one of the internal contradictions of The System.

Our hope is that a rational reorganization of political systems, bringing them into closer correspondence with current perceptions of social realities, may be possible without violence. Although this means taking it all apart and putting it back together, rehabilitating the entire structure of government for the people who inhabit the increasingly urban land masses, and would of necessity require the recovery of power from those who now hold it, there are many reasons why this radical shift should be accomplished without violence, and only a few that argue for a violent change. In the first place the System, in most western countries, has accumulated so many contradictions, both internal and external, as to seriously impede its workings. Among these contradictions we may cite the illusory content of power, in western capitalism, where the only avowable ends to which it may be exercised are in the apparent public interest, leading to a continual transformation of the system toward pseudo-socialism. And since the power to further ends which are not avowable must be exercised clandestinely it grows increasingly vulnerable through disclosure. Another contradiction is that it is not apparent that any or all of the men in power really have the power to produce any radical change. Occasionally a super-powerful politician may appear, such as de Gaulle in the early sixties, who can organize enough support to effect constitutional changes. This is a rare occurrence indeed, and it should be noted in passing, marked an increase in the power concentrated in the hands of the national executive branch. Thus the only shift produced was in the sense of 'more of the same, only worse.' The logical extension of this trend toward more concentration of power leads to the absurdity of totally irresponsible and unresponsive autocracy. Further it may be argued that the uses of wealth in our capitalist system constitute a contradiction, and one which has been exposed by the presumed heirs in two ways: either they destroy themselves through its abuse, or they renounce it (almost) altogether in a search for more meaningful social action. There is today a movement toward change from our present system, in which the uncomfortably rich and the needlessly destitute are said to be 'structurally' necessary, i.e. essential to the functioning of the system, to one in which neither rich nor poor would be needed to play those demeaning roles. I believe that Continental City, and eventually Global City, are concepts which can lead from attitudes to actions, which would hasten that movement.

As we said before, the expansion and contraction of government, necessary to create the Continental City, would be accompanied by increasing community control over local affairs, such as schooling, health services, community facilities, real estate development (to the degree that it can be seen as of local interest) circulation within a given area, utilities and, of course, finances. Finance is the structure upon which the new system (like the old system) must be built.

How does a city finance itself? If the city is a continent, the methods can be worked out in an equitable manner, within that single economic unit which is vast enough to provide for all. The economic product is, by definition, sufficient to the needs of the society (the city). Indeed the economic product exists only as a function of society's needs. We do not have to concern ourselves with current financial practise, or the economic theories which have been used to justify the present state of obvious inequity. To know how the city, as we know it, finances itself is instructive mainly in that it radicalizes us. The only relevant theory may be Leontief's input–output analysis, but it cannot be applied with any credibility on the restricted scale of the existing city. When it is so used it becomes simply another weapon in the armory of oppression. Its promise is that it prefigures and can be used to organize a concept of national or continental economic units: the New City. Like most systems, it has a scale at which it works. It shows how the New City finances itself, but when applied, for instance, to Philadelphia it only serves to underscore the nonsensical idea of self-supporting cities. It probably would work best at the scale of the Global City, where it could show that the economic product is necessarily sufficient to the needs of society.

The notion of rich and poor countries disappears in the intent of a Global City, as that of rich and poor states is seriously shaken in the concept of the Continental City. How can we conceive of rich and poor when all are sharing and presumably all are productive? There are, to be sure, geographical areas which are potentially more productive than others, but it is inconceivable to allow that the inhabitants of the less productive areas, like inhabitants of London's Notting Hill, for instance, should be less affluent than the inhabitants of Mayfair or Chelsea, by reason of accidental location. The location is no accident, as we know, and it has very little to do with the productive potential of the land. The rich, who are rich through unspeakable means (why are they rich?) tend to congregate in certain quarters which they appropriate for reasons of amenity, and the poor are relegated to undesirable regions. The middle classes float between the two, ever striving to move toward the affluent quarters, which will no longer be affluent when they finally arrive. There is never any there there, when you get there. Upward mobility is a myth, a part of the bureaucrats' dream of controlled consumption. The Continental City concept can bring changes to that and other situations of gross inequity. To begin with, the land itself will, naturally, all be in public ownership. To follow, intelligent planning in the disposition of uses will eliminate the frenetic fluctuation of desirability which is current. All of the Continental City's land, i.e. all of the land, will be public property, and the distribution of uses can be reasonably determined, when necessary. Since there will be no private parcels, there can be no need for, or profit in, speculative manipulations of land value. Land has no value, *per se*. In the Continental City, we will have eliminated those private profit motives which in the past have proven to be counter-productive in the society's sense. This will be accomplished by municipalizing all the land, making it all public domain. After all, we all live here, and it is all ours, held in trust for our successors.

Having reconsidered our countries in this way, as rather large cities with vast under- or un-populated areas in them, we can now invent the methods of government and administration and finance which seem best suited to our new needs and desires, as citizens. This is indeed a formidable task, but perhaps the only one which seems worth undertaking. In conceiving of the Continental City, we will have shifted our social attitudes considerably from the tribal, territorial, quasi-animal impulses with which we are credited by a currently modish crop of anthropologists. Those attitudes have, of course, already shifted and no amount of nostalgic harking-back to Mother Africa will arrest our ambitions. The evolution of ideas and social attitudes is a force which cannot be countered, and therefore must be dealt with. Our tribes have long since been dissolved, and hunted-out territories abandoned. We've moved on to farms, cities, nations. We are perhaps ready for another move toward global consolidation, and the Continental City would certainly be a step in this direction. We would say then that relics of the past, on our social behavior, are at least partially balanced by intimations of the future.

The problems which are evoked in speculating upon the future of urbanism are so vast that one suspects that our immediate responses, on the whole, will be generally conservative. Mistakes from the past will be carried on into the future, mostly because it is always easier and more comfortable not to change. Change is frightening; the results are unknown. And, of course, the cumulative force of vested interests is formidable. When we propose a complete reorganization of political and financial structures, such as the Continental City, we are talking about revolutionary change. This is not, however, to say that such proposals should be dismissed because they are revolutionary. We need revolutionary attitudes, and I've attempted to show that revolutionary attitudes can perhaps lead to actions which are revolutionary in content without necessarily being violent in form; they are essential to counter the conservative forces which would argue for no change in an obviously disastrous situation. At present, time doesn't work for the cool-headed reformer, and gradual progress toward workable change for the better is less apparent generally than change for the worse. The promised fruits of reform have not been delivered or have turned out to be wax, and reform as a political attitude has been discounted prematurely.

Without some effective and broadly-based regional or continental administration which can act as a forum for decision-making, geographical location of new development will continue to be determined haphazardly and is liable to generate conflicts between semi-autonomous local interests and national or regional interests, or between minority rights and majority responsibilities. New development clearly should be related in intelligible ways to existing settlements and activities, in functional relationships which may or may not coincide with momentary political desiderata. Minority rights and majority responsibilities are the components of a valid compromise; neither can be entirely ignored. It is unlikely that any urban or regional planning action which overrides altogether the rights and demonstrable needs of a local minority can serve the best interests of the majority, since it would create or maintain areas of conflict which can only be harmful, in the long run, to the whole of society.

Now the establishment of community control on the one hand and national or continental planning action on the other, may not seem to provide, on the face of it, any better solutions than those which are currently available. However, we believe that the dissolution of national hierarchies and their replacement by a single city-wide, nation-wide planning agency would have the immediate and salutary effect of always placing regional or local urbanistic events and problems in a total social context. At the same time we think it would necessarily result in other national planning agencies, such as a national employment agency, which would in turn require the development and enunciation of national policies on employment, distribution of the economic base, etc. And naturally, the removal of intermediate hierarchies would reinforce the local community's need for local control and its desire to participate in the decisions which affect its physical and social environments.

Bresse-Revermont

In 1967 the French Ministry of Agriculture, awakening to the problems of rural dislocation, organized a national planning competition in which multi-disciplinary teams were invited to study the situation of certain disfavored regions where the land no longer supported the population living on it. The part of agriculture in the French economy has shrunk rapidly while the number of persons dependent upon agriculture decreased at a much slower rate over the decades since the First World War. After the Second World War the depopulation of rural regions tended to accelerate, as the increasingly impoverished small farmers gave up their rural pursuits. At the time of the competition about 18 per cent of the population was still statiscally agricultural, while agriculture accounted for about 8 per cent of the national product. Various vaguely social, piecemeal programs were tried, such as retraining the younger farmers to give them industrial skills, and providing pensions for the older ones. However, generally the economic situation of small farmers continued to deteriorate and, in the absence of a coherent national policy of employment, emigration from rural areas continued in a quasi-clandestine manner. The young migrated to the towns first, then to the cities, but neither town nor city was prepared to receive them. They could not remain on the land, in competition with large-scale agricultural corporations which had consolidated holdings on the richest soils. There was no place to go except to the city, and there there was neither lodging nor work. France had become over-populated, apparently, although cheap labor was still being imported from poorer places around the Mediterranean, such as Portugal, Spain and North Africa, and a national policy of increased birth-rate was being hawked by the government. The policy of the national government was completely incoherent, probably owing to the rigid compartmentation which characterizes autocratic bureaucracies.

In this context the competition was organized, ostensibly to solicit solutions from planners, architects, economists, sociologists, anthropologists, and others. The problem posed was: what should be done to revitalize and rehabilitate the poorest regions? The competition was limited to selected regions, for which suggestions were requested. It seemed obvious to us that the problem was badly stated, that the question was not one of regional, or local, development, but one of national policy.

We proceeded on that basis, and assumed that a national policy of productivity and employment would deal with the problem of rural impoverishment in a reasonable way. We chose to study the area called Bresse-Revermont, north of Bourg-en-Bresse, in the foothills of the Jura mountains. It is a region dotted with small farms (some

108. The area of Bresse-Revermont situated in the foothills of the Jura Mountains, about fifty miles NNE of Lyon. Map showing primarily agricultural regions of France.

109. *The competition was limited to selected regions, for which suggestions were requested. It seemed obvious that the problem was badly stated, that the question was one, not of regional, or local, development, but of national policy.* Bresse-Revermont in its economic region.

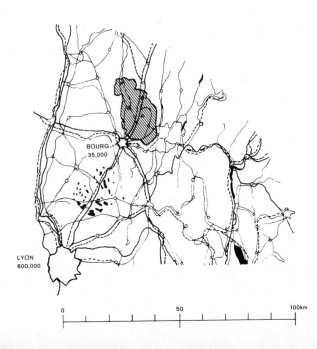

BOURG
35,000

LYON
800,000

0   50   100km

as small as ten to fifteen acres), and hamlets, in a pattern that has become today impossible to maintain. Dairy products and poultry are the principal exports of this region where virtually all rural activity is carried out on a small scale. It is poor and grows poorer although the old farm buildings convey a sense of bygone comfort and even a relative affluence. The aura of deterioration is one which has certain similarities with that which enshrouds the former African colonies of France. There existed here a viable society at some time in the past, before national policies, 'progress' rendered it unviable. The population of the area under study declined from 25,000 in 1870 to 10,000 in 1965.

We proposed to reorganize the area and its activities in several ways. One was to encourage, through initial subsidies, cooperative action by the remaining farmers. Another was to encourage a policy of centralization and regrouping of the hamlets and villages into more functional communities of a size which could hope to use modern systems of equipment and services. These new, almost urban, settlements were to be carefully grafted on to selected existing villages. They required national funding and a policy of national investment in certain light industries. Hydro-electric power is cheaply available in the region although distribution of power is costly. We also, almost incidentally, suggested that the potential for leisure activities for the inhabitants of Bourg, Lyon and Geneva might be expanded as a further means of support. But principally we were concerned with demonstrating the possibilities of a national policy, approaching the problem at its source rather than letting it escalate into greater problems both locally and nationally.

We reasoned that a social and economic cost–benefit analysis would show that it is more profitable to stimulate employment in the impoverished area than to displace the impoverished persons to already congested cities where they only enrich an already over-rich labor market and add to the load on an overloaded urban habitat. Certainly this approach would generate new forms of human settlement, and these would be much easier to organize in an undercrowded rural situation than would the further growth of Lyon and Paris.

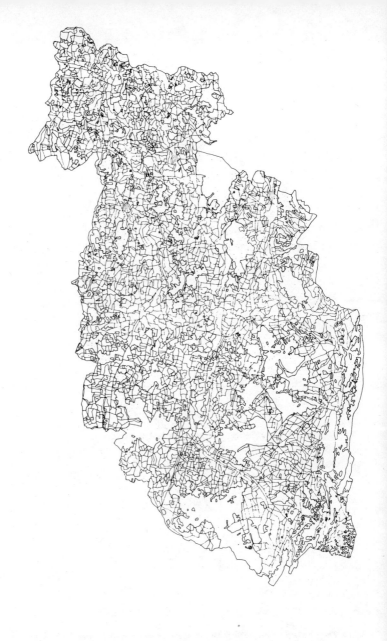

110. *It is a region dotted with small farms and hamlets, in a pattern which has become today impossible to maintain . . . It is poor and grows poorer.* Bresse-Revermont, area 60,000 acres, population 10,000. Map showing property lines. This scale belongs to the past.

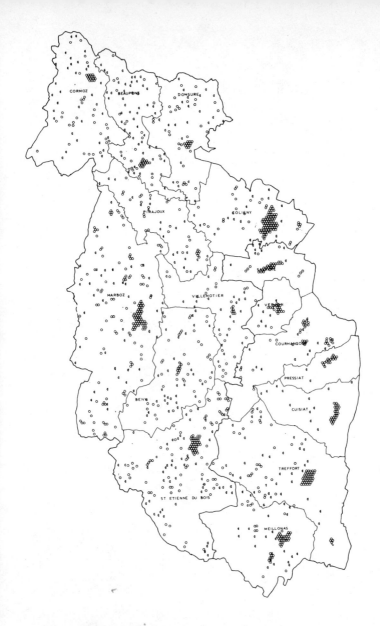

111. *There existed here a viable society at some time in the past, before 'progress' and national policy rendered it unviable.* Population distribution in Bresse-Revermont. Each dot represents ten persons. The population has declined from 25,000 to 10,000 over the past one hundred years. This also gives an image of built domain and indicates the difficulty involved in low-intensity distribution systems, were it proposed to rehabilitate the existing habitat.

112. *To encourage a policy of centralization regrouping of the hamlets and villages into more functional communities of a size which could hope to use modern systems of equipment and services.* Bresse-Revermont: Rural and urban development trends. (1) In the old order, prior to 1870, farms and hamlets were dispersed around a center for exchange. (2) 1900–present. With technological advances in agriculture and communications a disorganized migration toward the city takes place, leading to overcrowding of cities and under-equipment of rural areas. (3) 1940–present. Suburbanization: exodus of middle class leaving the city slums under-equipped. (4) 1970? A proposed new order in which activities and equipment are distributed in a new constellation.

There are still many more people living in rural areas than the agricultural sector of the economy can support. This proposal aims to bring some of the collective equipment (social, educational, cultural and commercial facilities), as well as some of the basic economic factors, to those who remain in the rural areas, and to slow, and eventually stop, the migration toward the cities. As agriculture becomes an industry the agricultural worker can become a city dweller. The new cities thus created would also help to regulate the disorganized growth of the existing cities. A more satisfactory mix of urban and rural could be achieved, especially in these new quarters of the national city.

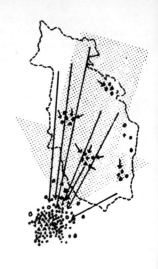

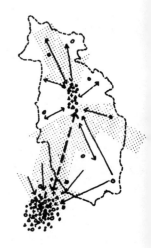

Unfortunately, it transpired that what the organizers of the competition had in mind was not a solution to a grave problem but a kind of innocuous do-goodery along the lines of development of cottage industries which could be activated in small increments when required for electoral purposes. There was to be no national policy for investment, employment or planning. Nothing has been done, to date, to alleviate the problems of rural dislocation and urban congestion in France, and those of us who thought we saw an opportunity to expose the problem, at least, have been only exposed as the naive fools that we are. Clearly it is not the business of national governments, as we know them, to elucidate national policies effectively.

Bresse-Revermont in France, like New York City in America, will continue to decline, to decay, to deteriorate. Both are victims of a non-sensical non-policy of national non-planning. Lawyers and bankers assure us that this is for the best, that free enterprise is the

113. Bresse-Revermont: The four hypotheses for future development in the area. It is assumed that the state will undertake to complete the social and educational equipment in the area. In that case, where should the major effort be concentrated, or should it be diffused? With such a dispersed habitat as exists here currently, it is not conceivable to scatter elements of equipment of any reasonable size. They should then be grouped, with other activities, either in small or larger existing centers. One possibility would be to choose the greatest existing pole of attraction. i.e. the city of Bourg-en-Bresse, which has the disadvantage of being excentric to the area. A second possibility would be to attempt to develop the existing villages, spreading the new equipment among several small centers. This was deemed to be expensive, both initially and in terms of efficiency of operation and transportation loads. In addition it creates a climate of political competition and jealousy. The third possibility is to concentrate all equipment in one of the largest existing villages, St Etienne du Bois. However it was thought preferable to develop a new center, more centrally located in relation to all the existing villages so that the new investment could be made easily accessible to all within the region. This rural new town would be located on a site near the center of gravity, on the edge of a new lake which was proposed to stabilize the hygrometric system of the best potential farming land.

salvation of man, but Bressans and New Yorkers remain unconvinced. If it were true, it would surely be apparent.

Planning, we can see clearly, is not an activity well thought of in western countries. Physical planning requires economic planning and economic planning is anathema to our established systems of exploitation. City planning of some sort, however timid, has become in this century a necessity. The planning of regions around and between cities, regional or national planning, naturally follows but resistance builds and it is by no means certain that effective regional planning (as opposed to piecemeal making do) will see the light in our time. Until it does, we shall all remain victims, manipulated and oppressed by the very systems which we are supposed to be controlling.

Continental City may appear to be a witticism, but we urge that it be examined seriously. It may be the only way in which we can hope to extend (city) planning to the national scale. In a desperate situation, any hope is better than none.

114. Bresse-Revermont: Implantation and projected growth of a new urban entity. This new center would be not only oriented toward the agricultural activity surrounding it but would also provide an economic base for those who are obliged to leave the land. Included in its basic activities are primary and secondary education, administration, medical and social services, commerce, professional and agricultural services, cultural and religious activities, leisure and tourism.

The new city would be located on a lake which we proposed to create. An industrial complex is proposed for north of the lake. (Project for Bresse-Revermont by Woods, Baboulene, Courtas, Cropier, Darre, Dosse, Piot, Poupon & Renoud with J. Pfeufer.)

5. The Global City

Now that transportation and communications between the continents, countries and cities of the world become ever more rapid and virtually no place where men live remains remote from another, when the globe has shrunk to an apprehensible size, we are obliged to take a new view of the economic, social and political systems which our societies have inherited.

There is no more *terra incognita* on earth; we cannot solve or elude our problems by striking out into new territory. The size and shape of our planet are known, and we know also pretty well what its resources of energy and materials are. In any case we know that they are not unlimited, although no limit to the numbers of persons who must share them is yet clearly in sight.

A new context of urbanism has been established through these realizations. At the same time that scientists have evaluated the total global wealth in existing and potential natural resources, other scientists have predicted a two-fold increase in population over the next generation approximately (taking the old measure of time, one generation is about thirty years). Others have found that the increasing exploitation of natural resources, especially petroleum and relatively rare metals, is destroying at an increasing rate the natural environment and disrupting the ecological cycles which keep the world and its population alive. They are all convincing in their statistics, although not so much in their conclusions, which rely on the logical projection of those statistics into the future. The world will certainly not perish from over-population although it may seem seriously threatened by the ecological side-effects. The population will undoubtedly decrease as ecological stress increases. Some would then be led to question the bases as well as the processes of these exact sciences, such as actuarial prediction, and might tend to think wishfully about the world's future and thus to discount today's problems. The data with which we are supplied, indeed inundated, concerning the future should however not be ignored. We must include them in our picture of the context of urbanism today, the potential of which we seek to discover. We rebel naturally at projections which offer no hope, and we may tend to overcompensate. Like Duchamp, we say (and would like to think) 'There is no solution, therefore there is no problem.' But there is a problem; there are many problems, and there may be many solutions, most or all of which do not conform to logical or ideological premises. Nonetheless these data, however questionable, have become one of the essential ingredients of urbanism. The world may not end either with a bang or a whimper, indeed we must assume that it will not if we are to proceed intelligently and effectively in our pursuit of global urban integration. Our assumption that structural changes will avert the final disasters should not, however, blind us to the urgency of change.

Urbanism will continue to concern itself primarily with today more than with unpredictable futures, since its nature is to be immediate, i.e. to operate from existing situations. At the same time, urbanists will be concerned with long-range planning, with concepts underlying continuing change as well as decisions to accommodate immediate change. They will then be influenced by the data which are furnished by those whose science it is to study and to project trends in human societies, especially global trends. Policy, in urbanism as elsewhere, cannot be made only out of tradition and good intentions. Policy-makers seek, and are receptive to, all kinds of information and opinion, including the software of the futurible.

We are aware now that the world is an entity. The diverse and isolated worlds of the past have grown together into one agglomeration. 'The world,' as Roger Vailland said, 'at the scale of the universe, is an island.'* Vailland was extrapolating from his investigation of the island of La Réunion, in the Indian Ocean, which exemplified to him many of the ecological and economic abuses which the world suffers. An increasing population living on decreasing resources

* In *La Réunion* éditions Rencontre, Geneva, 1964.

as a result of poor management of the land, turned the island from a paradise (as seen through eighteenth-century eyes) into a prison of hungry people. There is no longer any excuse for poor management, but on La Réunion it may be too late to reverse the march of progress, which created an ecological imbalance in order to sweeten the coffee of the French. Forests were cut indiscriminately to plant cane; erosion washed the earth into the sea; cane consumed the soil.

In the past we could, like the French planters on La Réunion, consider separately the discreet areas or segments of the world, built and unbuilt. Today such an attitude appears inconceivable to anyone who wishes to retain his humanity. Technological progress has shrunk the world and we must adjust our ethics to the measure of our technologies. Our urbanistic philosophy is governed by global social concern. All the people in the world are directly concerned in the allocation and use of the world's wealth. We are all passengers on what Bucky Fuller calls 'Spaceship Earth,' all inhabitants of Vailland's island. The urbanist is one of those who assume responsibility for directing the use, or misuse, or conservation of the world's resources, directly or indirectly. He is then naturally involved with the global effects of his local decisions, as he is concerned with the efficient and equitable use of those resources. He is one of the engineers on the spaceship.

The current projection, with which we must reckon, shows the number of passengers doubling in a little more than a generation. It is said, with hope, in academic circles that dwindling resources can and will be replaced by increasing skills. But the best milker cannot get more than the udder will give, and in any case this theory would scarcely constitute a logical basis for continuing to waste the planet at an increasing rate. Injudicious exploitation can, as on La Réunion, irreversibly affect the ecological system.

The current reality, as far as we can apprehend it, seems to constitute a convincing accusation of western civilization. Barbara Ward estimated that 30 per cent of the world population is consuming 80 per cent of the world product. One can travel first class as well as steerage on the spaceship. The supplies are raided by crafty stewards for the exclusive delectation of a minority: us. And all this is accomplished through violence. We should act soon, in the hope of forestalling further violence, to reintegrate our family of fellow-passengers as equal members. There is a need for equilibrium between the general good and the particular advantage. Perhaps both are necessary components of a functioning system, but if the system is out of balance, as it seems to be, it will run wild, to the detriment and eventual destruction of all, in a welter of violence.

If we are to understand anything about urbanism and its objectives, we must try to relate it to the economic state of the world. The world is much preoccupied with materialism. We feel very deeply the need to dominate matter, so deeply that it almost excludes all else. We must then face up to the material situation in the world. We can perceive a chain of facts which calls for a change of attitudes. First, the natural wealth of the globe at any given time is limited; second, there does not seem to be any limit to the population of the globe; third, the present distribution of the world's wealth is dangerously inequitable, and the projected distribution even more so. (At the present rate, the UN estimates it will take about 300 years for Africa to achieve parity with the 'developed' continents.)

We may conclude from these observations that, in the interest of life on earth (in which we all are interested) we are all involved in and concerned with a critical situation. The trips that prime ministers and presidents take to third world countries may be construed either as continuing colonialism or as new global concern. They are somehow encouraging, whatever the motive, since they imply recognition (or force recognition) of a problem. We can say that urbanism, being concerned with the use of the world's wealth, is always of global importance, no matter where it may be practised. The whole world is a city, and urbanism is not only the organizing of a local physical environment for the best accommodation of people's activities and tranquillities; it is also the equitable and efficient allocation, use and replenishment of the world city's wealth. Clearly, as in nature so in art; inefficient or unevenly loaded systems will fail to perform, will jam or break down. Irrational concentrations of wealth and power will destroy those who presume to profit from them. I would say that all concentrations of wealth and/or power are irrational, since they can only produce inefficient systems dependent eventually on a single, overloaded line of decision. Hence the proposal for global municipalization, with diffusion of power within a coherent web of decision and responsibility.

We see then that the concerns of urbanists are increasingly global. The global village of Marshall McLuhan is really a global city. We have long been considering urban regions as distinct entities (the East and West coasts of the US, the Ruhr, the Benelux countries, etc.) and we have gone from this to regarding countries or continents as cities with rather large open spaces in them. We could well go on to understanding and accepting the planet as a single city-organization. And just as we say that all the activities which might sustain life in the city can and should co-exist in an harmonious entity, so should all the activities and wealth of the world be sensibly allocated.

The physical form of the global city, the geometry of its web of communications, the constellations of points of intensity of activity, of production and exchange cannot be predetermined. Those constellations are constantly shifting; the web deforms and reforms itself to accommodate them.

Concepts of physical organization in urbanism are usually quite simple. They are derived from the laws which govern the physical world, such as the law of motion, from observation of human reaction to environments, or from easily understood topological theorems. They have to do with fitting many things together while yet assuring access to all of them and between all of them. Thus the street, the web of streets, patterns of public and private domain in two or three dimensions are easy to understand and to use. Laying out an urban system for purely physical functioning is a pretty simple task although its very simplicity makes it an extremely difficult one. For when we reduce things to their simple expression we invariably discover how much complexity we have concentrated into that simplicity. There are complexities which simply will not distill out of the problem, like salt in the sauce, no matter how much we reduce it. However, we can resolve the complexities within the simplicity of physical systems in good or bad ways without calling into question the systems themselves. We establish a base on which to build and that, at least, is an affair within the compass of our competence.

When we seek to go beyond the organization of an immediate urban context however, we must change from simple physical concepts to complex political and financial ones. Although we can easily envisage leaping from the local urban scene to the continental complex of urban, rural, forest and desert zones, as a problem of physical organization, we still must recognize that the problem is not only, and usually not even, one of physical organization. Certainly the infrastructure of roads and piped and wired services is purely physical, but the superstructure of human relationships escapes any simple systematization. Forces beyond our comprehension enter into play, even at the city scale. How much more powerful are those unreasoning atavistic forces of territoriality, xenophobia and conservatism at the continental scale.

What hope may we have then of transposing these problems of urban organization to the global scale? It is clear that we should, in the interests of survival, at least begin to consider the planet as a single entity, in terms of resources and life-support systems. Logically we would then proceed to develop a unified political system, and thence to organize it as a single administrative unit: the Global City. The theory is attractive, but what shall we do with all of those countries and nations, and their vast reservoirs of national pride and identity? Obviously nearly everyone on earth (i.e. in the future Global City) considers himself better, by reason of geographical or tribal origin, than everyone else on earth. Is it possible to convince him that he is not superior by simple virtue of racial background, and that the Global City is a valid idea? Certainly it is possible; all is possible, but what an extraordinary amount of persuasion will be required! Persuasion has never been a dominant force in global affairs.

The world is already, in effect, a city, with events in Johannesburg influencing life in Tokyo, just as events in Whitehall influence life in Chelsea, or events in Washington influence life in New York. It only remains to persuade people to recognize these facts, and to take their planetary destinies into their own hands. The secret dreams of global domination, which seem to haunt most nations, would be laid to rest, since all nations would have their share in global domination, i.e. in cultivating the world for the greater good of all people on earth.

We certainly need to realize collectively that the world is finite in its resources, although infinite in its possibilities. The population-bomb scare worries us, but we are really concerned with the need for global parity, the conservation of the biological environment and the improvement of the physical and psychological milieu in which we all must live. Most of us who are concerned with the state of the world today (the real world, not the world of power diplomacy *à la* Metternich) are not too much preoccupied with power and prestige and the perquisites which accompany them. In our image of ourselves we are much concerned with the realization of those schemes which we believe to be relevant and beneficial to the world at large. We know, or think we know, that the world is not going to end, but to continue. We may envy the poet who can sense the still point of a turning world but our instinct seems to be to turn with the world, not to seek the still point, to participate, not to observe.

We may now believe in man's potential for complete control over the planet and its resources, but we do not yet understand that the human resources of the earth are part of its wealth, nor how those human resources are to be nurtured and husbanded. The peoples which seek domination, essentially the white, have not yet been able to conceive of a world in which they could live in peace and amity with the other races which populate the globe. In the west we still think, despite our knowledge of the material situation of the world, in the same old stereotypes of power blocs and balances of payments and global domination. We have only begun to perceive, dimly, that these patterns of thought no longer fit the situation, that equity, not domination, is the only reasonable future. Where do we go from here? The planet (spaceship Earth) is still a marvelous place, full of people and loaded with the resources needed to support them. We need to imagine a planetary system in which their mutual support is assured. The world is rich, but to establish and maintain a global economy, sufficient to our numbers, we will have to rid ourselves of the present systems of exploitation of its wealth. We can continue to destroy the world piecemeal, as we have been doing in the name of peace, or we can decide to live with it, as well as in it, and that may well mean a serious reduction in our material 'standard of living', which may or may not affect the quality of life adversely. In any case we can say that continued mystification, such as the dogma of economic expansion or the absolute rightness of political creeds, will get us nowhere, in urbanism or in other necessary planning activities, and the recognition of that fact may already be the largest step that we can take along the road which might lead to global consciousness.

There are conclusions to be drawn from this polemic. We've tried to show that urbanism, in evolving from an art of émbellishment, demonstrates the need to extend both its physical scope of services and its political horizons. In a few generations we have grown to the realization that urban problems are world problems. No city is an island, anymore. To deal with the problems of the city is to become immersed in the problems of the world, in the use of its resources and thus, finally, in the political systems which manage and allocate those resources. The world is an island.

Urban planning determines the future use of resources of energy through the efficiency of operation of the systems which it establishes. The energy resources of the world are not yet limited in their quantity as new energy sources are exploited. However, every use of available energy is accompanied by an increase in ambient pollution, either locally or elsewhere, or both. This fact places environmental planning in a global context from which it cannot escape. Planning and programming for urban systems of transport and distribution of goods and services are activities with more than local importance, since they determine future commitments to the consumption of energy.

In a similar way, design of buildings, and especially of complex buildings such as pieces of cities, or extensions to them, determine a use of materials which has both social and economic implications at the local and global levels. The use of manpower, of skilled, semi-skilled, and unskilled labor in construction has immediate local and regional impact. In addition, specifying the use of certain materials

Con
Edison
salutes
the
World
Trade
Center.
More
power
to
it!

115. *Every use of available energy is accompanied by an increase in ambient pollution, either locally or elsewhere, or both. This fact places environmental planning in a global context from which it cannot escape.* Advertisement taken by New York power supply company in a newspaper supplement devoted to the World Trade Center in lower Manhattan. The World Trade Center adds some 12 million square feet of commercial and office space to a saturated market in an overcrowded area. More pollution for no discernible return.

116. *In addition, specifying the use of certain materials may have more far-reaching implications than we might at first suspect. This is especially the case, for instance, with exotic metals which are mined in the other hemisphere.* Strip mining for copper in Katanga.

may have more far-reaching implications than we might at first suspect. This is especially the case, for instance, with exotic metals which are mined in the other hemisphere. These observations have become banal.

If it is not yet glaringly obvious that what we do in making the urban environment eventually affects everyone in the world, it is becoming more and more clear to us that this is indeed the case. We've catalogued the resources of the globe, and are becoming aware that the greatest resource of all is people, they who generate the energy potentials which eventually concentrate and coalesce into policy. At the scale of the universe, policy is survival at the least, and, for the greater number, improvement of the conditions of life. To the realization of that policy we should all be devoted.

The world is a city, and urbanism is everybody's business.

Index

Page numbers in *italics* refer to illustrations.

Vailland, Roger, 215
Van der Rohe, Mies, 65
Venice, canal pollution, *39*
Versailles, 5, *5*, 8
Vested interests, 61–2, 74, 195
Violence, change by, 198–9, 202, 217
Virgil, 93

Wagner's *Rheingold*, 75
War
continental cities and, 194
Departments, 196
economy, 74
Ward, Barbara, 216
Waste of resources, 75
Water supply, 38
Wealth
city, outflow exceeding inflow, 22
distribution of, 188 (*see also* Poor;
Poverty)
inequitable, 42, 82, 107, 186–7,
199, 216–18

power and, 186
world city's, 217
Weil, Simone, 159
West
colonialism in, 81–2, 91–2, 186,
196
policies of, 220
White man's conscience, 116
Wilmington (California), 40
World
as city, 189, 199, 200, 214–24
as entity, 216, 219
domination of, 220
future of, 214–15, 220
World Trade Center, 50, *222*
World War, Second, *84*

Xenophobia, 219

Zoning, urban, 11, 54–5, 57–8, *59*,
72–3, 137, 153–4, 157, 160,
168

S. KATHARINE'S COLLEGE
LIBRARY